Hiking Central Florida

A Guide to 30 Great Walking and Hiking Adventures

M. Timothy O'Keefe

FALCONGUIDES ®

GUILFORD, CONNECTICUT
HELENA, MONTANA

FALCONGUIDES®

Text design by Nancy Freeborn
Maps created by Multi Mapping LTD © Rowman & Littlefield
Interior photos © M. Timothy O'Keefe

Library of Congress Cataloging-in-Publication Data
O'Keefe, M. Timothy.
  Hiking central Florida : a guide to 30 great walk-ing
        and hiking adventures / M. Timothy O'Keefe.
       p. cm. – (Falconguides)
     ISBN 978-0-7627-4354-4

1. Hiking–Florida–Guidebooks. 2. Trails–Florida–
Guidebooks. 3. Florida–Guidebooks. I. Title.

 GV199.42.F6054 2009
 796.5109759–dc22

2008039473

Distributed by NATIONAL BOOK NETWORK

To Jeff, Carolyn, and David Butler.
Sharing the outdoors with all of you for so many years
was always the high point of living in Central Florida.
Carrie, we miss you.

HELP US KEEP THIS GUIDE UP TO DATE

Every effort has been made by the author and editors to make this guide as accurate and useful as possible. However, many things can change after a guide is published—trails are rerouted, regulations change, techniques evolve, facilities come under new management, etc.

We welcome your comments concerning your experiences with this guide and how you feel it could be improved and kept up to date. While we may not be able to respond to all comments and suggestions, we'll take them to heart, and we'll also make certain to share them with the author. Please send your comments and suggestions to the following address:

The Globe Pequot Press
Reader Response/Editorial Department
P.O. Box 480
Guilford, CT 06437

Or you may e-mail us at: editorial@GlobePequot.com

Thanks for your input, and happy trails!

Contents

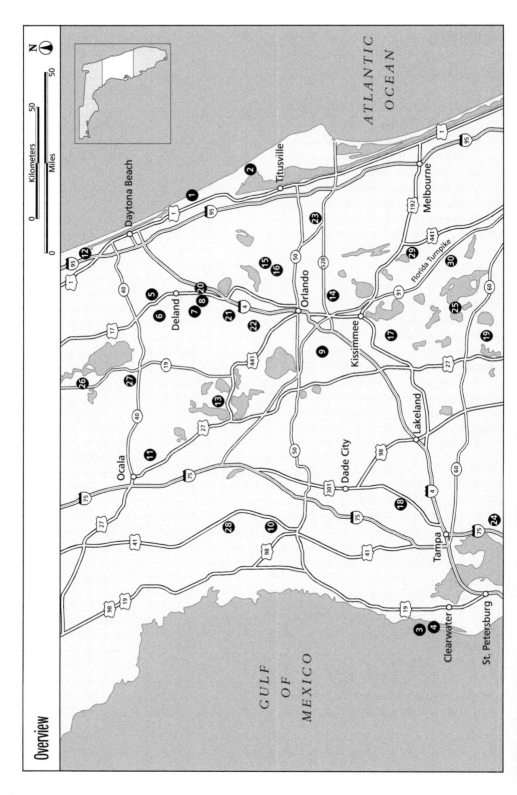

Overview

Acknowledgments

A guidebook to Central Florida hiking is possible only because of the untiring efforts of the Florida Trail Association, the volunteer organization responsible for creating and maintaining many of the state's best wilderness hiking trails, including the Florida National Scenic Trail (also known as the Florida Trail and FNST).

Also responsible for opening up and conserving hundreds of miles of Central Florida pathways are the staffs and volunteer helpers of the Florida Park Service, the state and national forests, and the state and national wildlife refuges and preserves.

These are the people who make it all possible for the rest of us. After every hurricane, they have a tremendous workload and do a terrific job.

Preface

No mountain high enough, no valley low enough…
what Central Florida hiking is like

Almost all of the thirty Central Florida trails described here are true hiking experiences on trails not shared with cyclists, skateboarders, and, in most places, horses, whose residual presence is not always appreciated in our hot Florida climate. Our definition of "Central Florida" extends from Ocala to State Road 60 near Lake Wales and Yeehaw Junction. However, two hikes described fall outside these boundaries: The northern section of the Florida Trail in the Ocala National Forest and the Bulow Plantation/Bulow Creek hike on the Atlantic coast. Those walks are generally thought of as part of Central Florida hiking; and they are just too good to leave out.

Walks in Central Florida can be as brief, or as long, as you wish. Many nature walks are quite short, taking only an hour or two. If that seems too tame, you can tackle several hundred miles of the 1,400-mile-long Florida Trail, one of eight National Scenic Trails. The unbroken stretch starting in the Ocala National Forest and ending south of Lake Wales can keep you occupied for weeks at a stretch as it winds through miles of thick forest and wetland nature reserves.

The thirty hikes described here are designed to highlight some of the best natural areas throughout the region and fall into four different categories: Short Family Hikes ranging from 1 to 3 miles, Day Hikes from 3 to 12 miles, Overnight Hikes with easy walks to primitive campsites, and Long Haulers, true backpacking experiences that require a weekend to complete. You'll also find that my companion book *Hiking Florida* contains a number of other Central Florida hikes not mentioned here. For other regions of Florida, check out my other new books *Hiking South Florida and the Keys* and *Hiking North Florida and the Panhandle*.

Central Florida hiking is some of the easiest in all of North America. Florida, essentially a spit of sand between the Gulf of Mexico and the Atlantic Ocean, is an incredibly flat place. So you'll find no mountains to climb, no deep valleys to descend, no dangerous precipices to teeter on. Rolling hills do break up the flat landscape in a few places, but these mounds are hardly formidable. The highest elevation in the state is a stunted 345 feet above sea level. That puts almost all Florida hiking within the capabilities of anyone, from the youngest walker to the oldest. During the driest months—January to May—when the ground is hard, many of these trails are barrier free. Boardwalk nature trails at many of the state parks are well suited for wheelchairs year-round.

One point about Florida hiking that may trouble some out-of-state visitors: Your dog is not welcome on all trails. Some parks and recreation areas require that pets be kept on a leash and confined to a picnic or camping area, and pets may not be allowed to stay overnight. A number of recreation areas are off-limits to pets of any kind, under any condition, with the sole exception of guide/assistance dogs. You'll need to check the "Canine compatibility" details with each hike.

"Walking is virtue, tourism deadly sin."

—Werner Herzog, film director

Visiting hikers may wonder about alligators and snakes but poison ivy should always be on their radar. It grows everywhere, from the deep woods to the most open sunny hiilside.

Introduction

What You'll See

The Florida peninsula is believed to be the last part of the continental United States to rise from the ocean, making it the youngest region geologically. Only Alaska can claim a longer shoreline.

Central Florida is classified as a subtropical region, receiving between 53 and 65 inches of rain a year. Relatively flat with a few rolling hills, Central Florida may not have the eye-popping panoramas of Colorado or Utah, but its landscape is quite striking in subtler ways.

Central Florida topography is usually classified according to its dominant biological communities, typically broken down as follows.

Air plants are fascinating but they should not be removed or disturbed, only admired.

Biological Communities

Cypress Swamp: The tall, gnarly bald cypress tree festooned with gray Spanish moss is the classic image of Florida. Bald cypress swamps are usually found near rivers. The pond cypress, a second species, creates the cypress domes that occur on the prairies and in pine flatwood forests.

Only aquatic animals such as snakes, otters, and lizards can survive in cypress swamps flooded most of the year. Deer and wild hogs live in swamps inundated only seasonally. Wet or dry, cypress swamps also house a variety of other plants, such as ferns, bromeliads (air plants), saw grass, and pickerel weed.

Scrub Cypress: Most common to south Florida, scrub cypress swamps are much smaller than the above. Because vegetation is scant, animal life is correspondingly sparse. Alligators, deer, and wood storks are among the few residents.

Forest Swamps: Also known as floodplain forest, these swamps are wet only part of the year. They are dominated by hardwoods such as water oak, black gum, sweet gum, and water hickory, with bald cypress and cabbage palm usually mixed in. Floodplain animals include bobcats, turkeys, deer, squirrels, otters, snakes, ducks, and songbirds.

Hammocks: In Florida the term "hammock" applies to any significant grouping of broad-leaved trees. A prime example is the live oak/cabbage palm hammocks of Central Florida. The name comes from the Indian word meaning "shady place." All hammocks generally enjoy fertile soil, and the trees remain green year-round. Common animals are toads, flying squirrels, wood rats, and birds such as the flycatcher.

Salt Marshes: Most commonly found along the coasts, salt marshes can be mixed in with mangroves or exist as a separate community. Black rush and cordgrass are the dominant plants. When salt marshes extend into tidal rivers, they often merge with freshwater marshes to form a fertile transition zone. Saltwater marshes are typically rich in bird and animal life, including otters, raccoons, turtles, and snakes.

Freshwater Marshes: A blend of sedge, grass, and rush, freshwater marshes have standing water for two or more months out of the year. Land with a shorter period of standing water is classified as wet prairie. Freshwater marshes often house many endangered species. Look for wood storks, sandhill cranes, and Everglades kites. Alligators, wading birds and other waterfowl, frogs, turtles, and otters also thrive here.

Dry Prairies: These treeless plains contain grasses and saw palmetto, with live oak/cabbage palm hammocks and dome cypress occasionally punctuating the flat spaces. A dry prairie may seem a lifeless, barren place, but closer inspection may reveal a considerable number of animals. Look for burrowing owls, sandhill cranes, raccoons, and bobcats.

Pine Flatwoods: Pine flatwoods are the most common type of biological community in Florida, with three types of pine forests: Pond pines grow in wet conditions, longleaf pines in the higher and drier regions, and slash pines in the transition zone between the two. Although each forest type is dominated by its particular pine species, animal life is more diverse, including black bears, deer, bobcats, raccoons, gray foxes, squirrels, birds, and black snakes.

Sandhill Areas: Fire is common in these dry and sparsely populated regions due to the arid conditions. It sometimes eliminates the longleaf pines, which are then supplanted by turkey and red oaks. Animals that burrow to avoid heat—and to escape the frequent fires—are common here: Gopher tortoises, indigo snakes, and pocket gophers are characteristic. In old-growth forest communities, you may be fortunate enough to spot the endangered red-cockaded woodpecker.

What to Avoid

Flat, easy terrain is the big plus of Central Florida hiking. Regrettably, there are also a few seasonal factors that make walking not as enjoyable as it might be.

Thorns of the Trail

Heat and Humidity: By far, these are the two biggest drawbacks of Central Florida hiking. From June until as late as mid-November, the temperatures routinely soar into the 90-degree range, and it's often too hot to hike comfortably except during early morning.

How comfortable you are depends on the combined effects of humidity and air temperature. The National Oceanic and Atmospheric Association (NOAA) offers the following chart as a guideline.

Air Temperature	Percent Humidity									
	10%	20%	30%	40%	50%	60%	70%	80%	90%	100%
	Feels Like									
125F	123	141								
120F	116	130	148							
115F	111	120	135	151						
110F	105	112	123	137	150					
105F	100	105	113	123	135	149				
100F	95	99	104	110	120	132	144			
95F	90	93	96	101	107	114	124	136		
90F	85	87	90	93	96	100	106	113	122	
85F	80	82	84	86	88	90	93	97	102	108
80F	75	77	78	79	81	82	85	86	88	91
75F	70	72	73	74	75	76	77	78	79	80
70F	65	66	67	68	69	70	70	71	71	72

Summer humidity often falls into the 60 to 80 percent range, which is why Central Floridians usually limit their daytime summer activity to moving from one air-conditioned spot to the next. Locals like to label anyone over the age of twenty-five with a summer tan as a tourist or a recent transplant.

Mosquitoes: Saltwater mosquitoes are active year-round in coastal areas while freshwater mosquitoes are mostly limited to the summer/fall rainy season. Wearing a long-sleeved shirt and long pants and applying insect repellent is the best defense. Mosquitoes typically become most active around twilight, a good time to be off the trail, hiding in a tent or standing around a smoky fire.

West Nile Virus: West Nile virus, closely related to the St. Louis encephalitis virus, is in Florida. Despite all the publicity, the incidence of the virus is still rare. In 2007 the Centers for Disease Control and Prevention reported only three human cases in Florida, down significantly from previous years, and none for the first six months of 2008. In Florida, more people are killed by lightning annually than by the West Nile virus.

The CDC advises that the best protection against mosquitoes and other biting insects is an insect repellent containing DEET. In addition, spray your clothing with repellents containing permethrin or another Environmental Protection Agency (EPA)–registered repellent, since mosquitoes may bite through thin clothing. Do not

See what summer storms can do. This tree has a serious lean.

apply repellents containing permethrin directly to exposed skin or to skin under your clothing. For the latest information on the West Nile virus, visit www.cdc.gov/ncidod/dvbid/westnile/.

Lightning: Frequent thunderstorm activity ranks Florida as one of the world's lightning capitals. In Central Florida you're more likely to be zapped by lightning than fatally bitten by a rattlesnake (which are at their liveliest in summer). July and August are peak lightning months, but expect frequent thunderstorms in June and September.

When a thunderstorm approaches:

- Stay away from the beach or any type of water.
- Try to get through the storm in a low spot under a thick stand of small trees.
- Avoid tall trees in open fields, trees at the water's edge, or trees whose roots are in damp soil.
- Don't shelter under oaks or pine trees. Because of their high starch content, they are among the best natural conductors of electricity.
- If you're wearing an aluminum-frame backpack, take it off—and stay well away from it until the storm passes.
- Stay away from wire fences or any pieces of metal that could conduct lightning to you.
- A tingling sensation in your scalp is a warning that a bolt may be about to strike: Fall to the ground immediately.

Hurricanes: Called "hurrican, the evil spirit" by the Indians, these storms can affect hiking conditions. Hurricane season begins in June, with the greatest activity typically in August, September, and October. As the saying about Florida's hurricane season goes: "June too soon, July stand by, August and September remember, October all over." The jingle is out of date as hurricanes have on rare occasion also appeared in November.

Hunting Season: Hiking is forbidden in some areas during the first week of the hunting season starting in November and also the period between Christmas and the New Year, when hunting is at its peak. The rest of the hunting season, hikers must wear a fluorescent orange vest (available at sporting goods stores). Never wear anything white—the white-tailed deer is the favorite target. Weekdays normally see the fewest hunters in the woods. Trails located in hunting areas are identified in the description section.

Dehydration: By far, this is the greatest danger you'll probably face when hiking in Florida. Thirst, dry lips, and a parched throat all are signs of dehydration. To maintain your energy:

Consume liquids even when you're not thirsty.

Maintain the proper potassium level (take supplements from health food stores, drink tea, or eat bananas)

Avoid colas and alcohol. They are diuretics that could dehydrate you even more.

Take advantage of air-conditioning. You will probably feel more rested if you sleep in an air-conditioned room following any extended hike.

Prickly Heat: In constant humidity, it's easy to develop a rash. Avoid rashes by powdering yourself in the morning and evening with talcum powder or powder containing zinc. Also wear loose-fitting pants. The most comfortable shirts for hiking are usually made of lightweight cotton.

Sunburn: Except for extreme elevations, Florida's sun is far more intense than anywhere else in the continental United States. Gradual exposure to the sun is essential. So is wearing a water-resistant sunblock (SPF 25 to 30). The best protection is to cover your skin with a long-sleeved shirt and long pants and to wear a broad-brimmed hat.

Untreated Water: In general, no water along Florida trails is safe to drink. Don't let clarity fool you: If you use spring or river water for cooking, boil it about five minutes to kill all parasites. Or use a filter designed to remove all parasites, including *Giardia*.

Intestinal Problems: Such afflictions are usually the result of a bacterial infection or from consuming strange food and drink. Always carry your own water, and avoid drinking from streams, no matter how clear/clean they look.

Poisonous Plants: Poison ivy and poison sumac are a problem in Florida as they are in much of the country. Touching either can produce a skin irritation that may develop small, itchy blisters. Poison ivy is a shrub that grows both upright and on the ground; it is characterized by leaves comprising three leaflets and berries that are often whitish. Poison sumac is a bush with leaves comprising seven to thirteen leaflets and white berries. Cortisone cream is an effective remedy for both.

Hypothermia: This dangerous condition most often occurs in the 30-to-50-degree air temperature range, so it's definitely a consideration even for sunny Central Florida. Hypothermia typically occurs on the trail when a hiker gets wet, then is exposed to a cold and chilly wind. Hypothermia sets in as the body loses heat faster than it is able to produce it.

The most effective treatment for hypothermia is to get the victim out of wet clothes and into dry ones. Have the person put on a hat, since as much as 80 percent of a person's body heat is lost through the head. Give the victim warm liquids (but not coffee, tea, or anything else containing caffeine) and have him or her sit by the fire. If a warm sleeping bag is available, have the person crawl into it. One of the most effective things to block out the cold, even if the person is still in wet clothes, is a "space blanket"—a thin piece of lightweight fabric that has remarkable heat-reflecting capability.

Getting Lost: Most Central Florida hiking trails are clearly blazed, so getting lost may require some concerted effort. Always carry a map, a compass, and a whistle (three blasts is the universal call for assistance), plus a flashlight in case you don't make it back before dark. And your cell phone.

The Rogues' Gallery: Animals & Insects

Rabid Raccoons: This designation isn't meant to be humorous but to drive home the point that sometimes rabies is a problem in Central Florida. Animals that are overly friendly or aggressive and that seem to have no fear of humans are definitely suspect.

Chiggers: These small red mites are fond of attacking around the ankles, waist, and wrists, where they burrow under the skin and cause severe itching. Putting clear nail polish on the chigger bites will often smother any critters still in the skin. Calamine lotion helps relieve the itching.

Fire Ants: Fire ant mounds are readily spotted—they look like shovelfuls of dirt. The danger is accidentally stepping on a mound and having the ants swarm up your legs. As many as half a million fire ants live in a colony. Anyone allergic to ant bites should carry appropriate medication, just in case.

Ticks: Because of Central Florida's warm weather, ticks are active almost year-round. Because of the danger of Lyme disease, it is essential to always use repellent in the woods and to check your clothing and body for ticks after a hike is over. When camping, spray your tent and sleeping bag with repellent. LYMErix, a vaccine against Lyme disease, is estimated to be about 80 percent effective.

No-see-ums: For the most part, only beach hikers at sunrise and sunset need to worry about no-see-ums, midges or sand flies so tiny they are almost invisible. Long pants and shoes and socks are the best protection.

Scorpions: Found most often in the dry regions of Central and North Florida, scorpions like to crawl into hiking boots at night. So shake out your boots, or keep them wrapped in your tent in a plastic bag. Scorpion stings are very painful, although they are rarely lethal.

Spiders: Although wolf spiders and jumping spiders can inflict painful wounds, only two species of spiders are a serious threat to humans: the black widow and brown recluse.

Black widows can be found in woodpiles, inside stone and wood walls, in outdoor toilets, and anywhere else that offers a good hiding place. A black widow bite requires an immediate visit to the hospital for antivenin, since about 5 percent of all black widow bites are fatal. The only other spider to be concerned about is the brown recluse, also known as the fiddleback or violin spider because of the distinctive violin-shaped marking on its back. The brown recluse is not deadly, but the venom from its bite actually causes body tissue around the inflicted area to disintegrate. Without medical treatment, the wound will continue to deepen and may take months to heal.

Snakes: Florida has a larger snake population than any other state, but snakes are rarely a problem if you stick to the trails, don't haphazardly step over logs without looking, and exercise common sense. Six Florida snake species are poisonous, and half of those are rattlesnakes: eastern diamondback rattlesnake, canebrake rattlesnake and pygmy rattlesnake. Others include the cottonmouth water moccasin, coral snake and copperhead (found mostly in the Panhandle).

The coral snake is related to mambas and cobras and is said to be the country's most poisonous snake. Fortunately, it is rarely a problem, since it must almost gnaw on a person to break the skin. Most bites occur when people pick up "the pretty snake" to examine it. Coral snakes make their homes in brush piles, rotting logs, and pinewoods. The coral is sometimes confused with the harmless king snake, which also has colorful markings. The way to tell the two apart: "Red touch yellow, kill a fellow; red touch black, won't hurt Jack." Not great poetry, but it makes its point.

If someone is bitten, the best treatment may be to do nothing except take the person immediately to a hospital. Cutting the skin and attempting to suck out the venom often does considerable harm, sometimes severing muscle tissue.

Alligators: This is last on the list of hazards, and for good reason. Unless you swim in a remote lake during the spring mating season, when alligators sometimes go a little crazy, or during low water levels, when they have been known to attack swimmers and even a lakeside jogger, gators should not pose a danger. Alligators normally run or disappear when they encounter a human unless they have been fed by people or you are accompanied by a dog (a favorite alligator snack). Never harass an alligator or get between the animal and its body of water.

Florida Trail Association

The first blaze for the Florida National Scenic Trail (FNST), or Florida Trail, was painted on a tree in the Ocala National Forest. It was the dream of a brand-new organization called the Florida Trail Association (FTA) to blaze a walkway running north-south through the entire state. They succeeded so well that in 1983 the Florida Trail was designated one of only eight National Scenic Trails by the U.S. Congress. Today, the Florida Trail System includes the linear 1,400-mile Florida Trail running north and south as well as another 300 miles of loop and linear trails not connected to the main trail.

The FTA is a group of dedicated hikers who still work hard maintaining the FNST. With eighteen chapters and almost 5,000 members, each year the FTA sends hundreds of volunteers to the woods to clear the way and preserve the vital system of tree blazes that lead hikers safely through the densest forest. About three-fourths of the 1,400-mile-long trail now consists of natural corridor. At completion, the FNST is expected to contain 1,800 miles of hiking trails. An estimated 1.8 million people walk some section of the trail each year.

Trail Blazes

Most of the blazes on Florida trails have been placed there by the FTA. The eye-level blazes are normally quite easy to spot. This is the FTA system:

- Orange blazes mark the main trail.
- Blue blazes designate side trails to developed campgrounds or a natural site of unusual interest. In some state forests, blue blazes mark the equestrian trail.
- White blazes mark the trails in many state parks.

Florida State Parks have twice won the National Gold Medal Award for excellence in Recreation Management from the National Recreation and Park Association, the only park system to be so honored.

- A double blaze signals a change in direction. It could also mean the trail is no longer taking the most obvious route. Don't leave a double blaze until you've spotted the next single blaze.

The FTA sponsors approximately 500 different activities that take place throughout the state each year. Members are kept informed through a bimonthly newsletter.

For information about joining, contact the Florida Trail Association, 5413 Southwest Thirteenth Street, Gainesville, FL 32608; (877) HIKE-FLA; www.floridatrail .org; e-mail: fta@floridatrail.org.

Florida State Parks

Perhaps the most underrated and underappreciated segment of the Florida outdoors is that managed by the state park system, which oversees the majority of the best day hikes and many outstanding natural areas. Florida State Parks manages 161 locations and adds new ones regularly as more land is purchased and put under protection. About 14 million people visit the state parks annually.

In 2005, for the second time in five years, Florida State Parks received the National Gold Medal Award for excellence in Recreation Management from the National Recreation and Park Association. This was the first time a state park system anywhere has received the recognition twice.

Camping in State Parks

About 50 of Florida's 161 state parks offer camping, with a total of more than 3,300 campsites. Reservations can be made up to eleven months in advance by calling (800) 326-3521 between 8:00 a.m. and 8:00 p.m. or visiting www.ReserveAmerica.com. Although the parks stay open until sunset year-round, you should check in between 8:00 a.m. and 5:00 p.m. Fees range from $12 to $28 according to park location, season, and whether you use water and electricity. Not all state parks accept pets in campgrounds. For parks that do allow pets, check out www.floridastateparks.org/CampCabinLodge.cfm. Look under "Pet Camping."

State Park Annual Passes

If you're going to spend considerable time in Central Florida's state parks, you'll probably want to investigate the annual entrance passes for individuals and for families of up to eight people. They are available online at www.floridastateparks.org/annualpass, at the parks, or through the mail by calling (352) 628-7002. The cost is $43.40 for an individual, $85.80 for families. Camping fees are extra. Any questions about Florida parks, including entrance fee schedules, can be answered by calling (850) 245-2157 or by visiting www.floridastateparks.org.

Hiking Techniques

Treading Lightly

Florida's warm weather and unique landscape are the main reasons so many people move to the Sunshine State. Central Florida in particular is in danger of being loved to death. As more and more land is developed into sites for homes, schools, and shopping malls, the forests and preserves become ever more precious. Although Central Florida may become ever more crowded, large sections of wilderness land must endure.

How you can help:

- Always stay on the designated trails.
- Leave wildflowers, air plants, and other foliage where you find them.
- Never walk on sand dunes.
- Camp only in designated areas.
- Be especially careful of campfires.
- Be careful of human waste. Bury it at least 6 inches deep, a minimum of 200 feet from any water and 100 feet from any campsite.
- Wash dishes at least 200 feet from streams and lakes.
- Don't leave unwanted souvenirs. Pack out everything.

Hiking with Children

In planning any outing with children, remember with whom you are hiking. Don't be surprised or upset when they act like kids. Five- and six-year-olds are often capable of hiking for short distances, but they are not apt to be prepared for all-day trips. A walk of an hour or two is a good way to introduce children to the outdoors.

Short nature walks like those at the front of this guide will have far more appeal than a simple two-hour jaunt through the woods where the fairly undramatic scenery doesn't change much. Interesting nature walks are the easiest way to create a life-long interest in the outdoors and all its diversity.

Encourage older children to carry their own packs. Some kids will want to bring favorite toys or books along. Children learn from their parents by example. Hiking and camping trips are excellent opportunities to teach young ones to tread lightly and minimize their imprint upon the environment.

How to Use This Guide

This book does not attempt to cover every trail in Central Florida. Instead, it is limited to thirty of the best and most varied Central Florida hikes that offer the chance to observe unspoiled, natural Florida at its finest. The maps are based on topographic maps issued by the state of Florida and those supplied by the USDA Forest Service and the state parks. And we used the DeLorme *Florida Atlas & Gazetteer* as an additional resource.

Unless you are making an extended hike over weeks along the Florida National Scenic Trail, you should find these maps adequate. For long-range hikes you may want to purchase a map from the Forest Service or the Florida Trail Association. Each trail is evaluated according to difficulty, but that is often based more on the length of the hike than the terrain conditions, which are normally quite flat.

However, these estimates may not take into account wet or muddy conditions resulting from prolonged rain or other natural events. These appraisals are only guidelines, subject to changing conditions, and should not be taken as unchanging gospel. Any time the weather has been unusually wet or dry, consult with the appropriate on-site agency listed with every trail. In summer and early fall, some trails routinely flood after heavy rains.

The marked distances should be taken only as guidelines, not precise absolutes. Although I sometimes walked with as many as three pedometers, it was rare that all three instruments agreed at every point of a hike.

Trail Finder Chart

Number	Hike	Fishing	Cabins	Primitive Camping	Campground	Swimming	Canoeing/Kayaking	Bicycling	Beach	Wildlife/Nature
1	Canaveral National Seashore	●		●		●	●	●	●	●
2	Merritt Island National Wildlife Refuge	●				●	●	●		●
3	Honeymoon Island State Park	●				●	●		●	●
4	Caladesi Island State Park	●			●	●	●		●	●
5	De Leon Springs State Park	●				●	●			●
6	Lake Woodruff National Wildlife Refuge	●		●				●		●
7	Hontoon Island State Park	●	●	●		●	●	●		●
8	Blue Spring State Park: Boardwalk		●	●	●	●	●			●
9	Tibet-Butler Preserve									●
10	Withlacoochee State Forest: McKethan Lake	●		●		●	●	●		●
11	Silver River State Park		●		●		●			●
12	Bulow Plantation Ruins Historic State Park	●					●			●
13	Flat Island Preserve			●			●			●
14	Split Oak Forest Mitigation Park									●
15	Geneva Wilderness Preserve									●

Number	Hike	Fishing	Cabins	Primitive Camping	Camp-ground	Swimming	Canoeing/Kayaking	Bicycling	Beach	Wildlife/Nature
16	Little Big Econ State Forest	•		•				•		•
17	Disney Wilderness Preserve									•
18	Hillsborough River State Park	•		•	•	•	•	•		•
19	Tiger Creek Preserve									•
20	Blue Spring State Park: Pine Island Trail	•	•	•	•	•	•			•
21	Seminole State Forest	•		•				•		•
22	Wekiwa Springs State Park	•		•	•	•	•	•		•
23	Tosohatchee Wildlife Management Area			•						•
24	Little Manatee River State Park	•			•		•			•
25	Lake Kissimmee State Park	•		•	•		•	•		•
26	Ocala North Trail	•		•	•	•	•	•		•
27	Ocala South Trail	•		•		•	•	•		•
28	Withlacoochee State Forest: Citrus Perimeter Loop			•				•		•
29	Three Lakes Wildlife Management Area: Linear Florida Trail			•						•
30	Three Lakes Wildlife Management Area: Prairie Lakes Unit	•		•			•			•

Map Legend

Transportation

Interstate Highway	═══(15)═══
U.S. Highway	═══(27)═══
State Highway	═══(19)═══
County Road	═══[CR27]═══
Dirt Road	= = = = =
Railroad	⊢—+—+—+—⊣
Featured Trail	▬ ▬ ▬ ▬ ▬
Other Trail	- - - - - -

Hydrology

Lake/Reservoir	
River/Creek	
Marsh/Swamp	
Mangrove Swamps	
Rapids	//

Land Use

Wildlife Preserve	
State Park/State Forest	

Symbols

Campground	▲
Point of Interest	■
Visitor Information	❓
Parking	🅿
Picnic Area	🌭
Ranger Station	🏠
Tower	🗼
City/Town	○
Trailhead (Start)	⑤
Bridge	≍
Restroom	🚻
Viewpoint	🔭
Interpretive Trail	🚶
Chapel	⚱
Scale	0 ——— Kilometer ——— 1 / 0 ——— Mile ——— 1

True North
(Magnetic North is
approximately 15.5° East) N

Short Family Hikes

TRAILHEAD

1 Canaveral National Seashore: Nature Trails

The 25-mile-long Canaveral National Seashore is the longest stretch of undeveloped beach on Florida's east coast.

The distance from the Florida/Georgia border to Key West is more than 500 miles. For all that distance, the longest stretch of undeveloped beach remaining on Florida's east coast is the 25-mile strip of barrier island known as Canaveral National Seashore.

When the Kennedy Space Center was developed on Merritt Island in the early 1960s, NASA found it had far more land than it needed. So, NASA invited two other government agencies to help manage the area. The U.S. Fish and Wildlife Service established the Merritt Island National Wildlife Refuge as a sanctuary for wintering waterfowl in 1963, and in 1975 the National Park Service created Canaveral National Seashore. The Seashore's close connection to the space program is still obvious: its southernmost boundary is in plain view of one of the space shuttle launch pads.

Start: Canaveral National Seashore is made up of three beaches: Apollo, Klondike, and Playalinda. Its four short nature walks all begin at Apollo Beach at the northern end.

Approximate hiking time: Four short hikes of 20 to 30 minutes each
Difficulty: Easy
Trail surface: Natural surfaces, including

oyster shells and sand. The Turtle Mound Trail is mostly boardwalk.

Seasons: Fall through early spring. Beware mosquitoes at sunset year-round; carry repellent.

Other trail users: Nature watchers, anglers

Canine compatibility: Pets not allowed

Land status: National seashore

Nearest town: New Smyrna Beach

Fees and permits: Entrance fee under $5

Schedule: The park opens at 6:00 a.m. year-round and closes at 8:00 p.m. April through October, at 6:00 p.m. November through March. The Visitor Information Center is open 9:00 a.m. to 5:00 p.m. daily except Christmas. The Center is located on the right, a little over a mile south of the entrance gate kiosk.

Maps: Provided at the entrance

Trail contacts: Canaveral National Seashore, HQ at 308 Julia Street, Titusville, FL 32796; (321) 267-1110. Also 7611 South Atlantic Avenue, New Smyrna Beach, FL 32169; (386) 428-3384. Visitor information recorded message (321) 867-0677; www.nps.gov/cana.

NESTING LOGGERHEAD TURTLES

The beachfront is far more than just a strip of sand, and what you'll view along the seashore walk changes with the seasons. In summer, the seashore is a vital nesting ground for endangered loggerhead and green sea turtles. Only daylight hiking is permitted, but special nighttime tours are conducted by the park service so visitors can watch the turtles lay their eggs. Early morning hikers may see a few stragglers. More likely all you'll spot are the turtle flippers' tread-like tracks leading down to the sea.

The turtles, particularly loggerheads, emerge from the sea to nest here between May and September. A female deposits as many as 120 eggs in the hole she digs with her hind flippers. She may repeat this procedure several times during the nesting season, yet only about one turtle from each of her nests will survive to adulthood.

Raccoons often eat the eggs, sometimes as soon as the turtle lays them. Shore birds pick off many of the hatchlings as they scamper toward the sea. Once the hatchlings reach the ocean, fish kill many more.

But this natural selection process is not what endangers the sea turtle population. Instead, bulkheads and beach developments have closed off old nesting grounds. Hatchlings, confused by street lights and other artificial illumination, go inland instead of toward the sea. As a result, many die of starvation or are killed by cars. Canaveral National Seashore is one of the most important turtle nesting grounds remaining on the east coast.

To join a guided turtle walk at night offered here and at other area beaches, visit www .floridawildlifeviewing.com and look under "Sea Turtles."

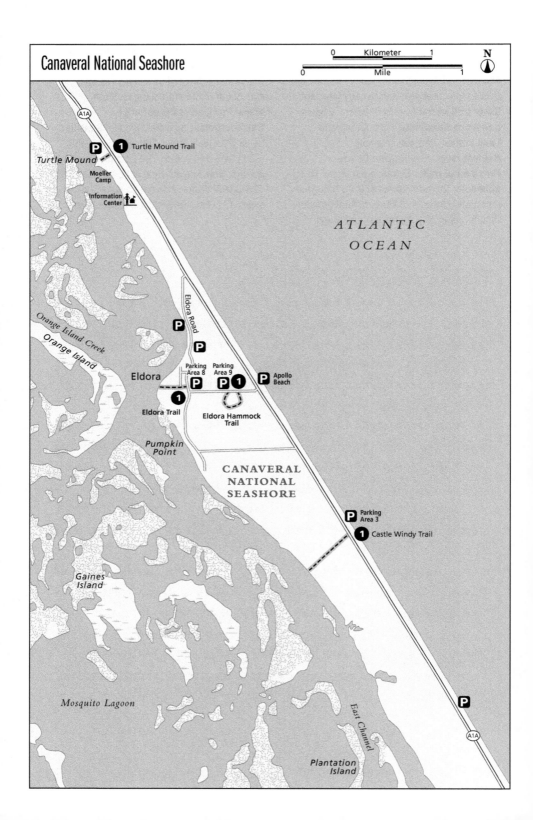

Finding the trailheads: Canaveral National Seashore's Apollo Beach is located 7 miles south of New Smyrna Beach about midway on Florida's east coast between Daytona Beach and Melbourne.

Apollo Beach is easily accessible from Interstate 95, Florida's major east coast highway. From I-95 take exit 249 onto State Road 44 toward DeLand/New Smyrna Beach and go east to New Smyrna Beach (about 20 miles). Just before the main downtown area, watch for the junction of SR 44 with Canal Street and Lytle Avenue. Turn right onto Lytle Avenue, which becomes Highway A1A and the South Causeway crossing over the Halifax River. Follow A1A for 7 miles south of New Smyrna Beach to the National Seashore northern entrance, at Apollo Beach.

All Canaveral National Seashore Nature Trails are located along Apollo Beach. The following walks are described from north to south in the order you approach them after entering the seashore.

Turtle Mound Trail

Finding the trailhead: Located 0.96 mile from the seashore entrance kiosk. Park on the right shoulder in the designated area. Take the boardwalk inland toward the Indian River. **GPS:** N28 55.832' W080 49.542'

The Hike

Turtle Mound is an ancient hillock of oyster shells left by the Timucuan Indians. A 0.25-mile, self-guided trail leads to the top of the two-acre shell pile. It apparently was created by oyster-eating Indians between 600 and 1200 A.D., possibly as a high-ground refuge during hurricanes. At 50 feet high, this is one of the tallest shell mounds remaining on Florida's east coast.

At one time the trail was built on the mound itself. These days, a boardwalk acts as a barrier to keep the shells from being trod on or picked over by souvenir hunters. The mound has never undergone a full archaeological excavation, and the plan is to protect it for future scientists to uncover more information about the Timucuans. The contents of other middens disclosed that Timucuans ate more than just shellfish, that their diet also included white-tailed deer and several types of small mammals and reptiles. Interpretive signs at several points explain their lifestyle in detail.

The Timucuans hunted and fished along the coast for almost 2,000 years. An estimated 40,000 of them lived in the region when the first Spanish settlers arrived. Their population was so dramatically reduced that most of the remaining Timucuans fled the state with the Spanish when they withdrew from Florida in 1763.

▶ The surf line is sometimes rich in shells, one of the few items you're allowed to collect here. The best time for shelling is immediately after one of the fall storms, when a fresh supply is washed ashore. The greatest varieties are found then, including razor clams, lightning whelks, calico scallops, and angel wings. The coquina clam tends to be the most common. It takes a fairly large number of these tiny 0.5-inch bivalves to make a decent chowder.

A popular daytime activity on the small beach here is to catch blue crabs using chicken necks and a small sinker tied to a stout piece of twine. The crabs become so involved in dining on the chicken necks they don't mind being reeled in like a fish—until they're scooped up in a long-handled net.

Miles and Directions

0.0 Start hike on boardwalk.

0.03 Reach open area with picnic table, no shade, and small beach on left. Continue straight to reach boardwalk bearing off to the right.

0.14 Boardwalk makes T, go right.

0.15 Reach platform section overlooking Indian River and facing New Smyrna Beach to the north. Retrace footsteps.

0.16 Boardwalk from picnic area comes in from the left. Go straight.

0.17 Reach second platform overlooking Indian River, facing south. Retrace footsteps.

0.18 Turn right on boardwalk to return to picnic area.

0.26 Arrive back at picnic area/beach.

0.37 Terminus at parking lot.

Eldora Trail

Finding the trailhead: Starts from Parking Area No. 8 on Highway A1A on the right, located 1.7 miles south of the Visitor Information Center. The trail starts at the southern end of the parking lot, near the kiosk and restrooms. **GPS:** N28 54.333' W080 49.066'

The Hike

The trail—less than 0.5 mile long—goes straight through a hammock to a small public fishing pier on the Indian River. It then turns left and skirts the river shoreline, almost immediately arriving at the impressive white wooden building called the Eldora State House. The State House, open to the public since 1999 and on the National Registry of Historic Places, contains exhibits and information about those who lived in the thriving town of Eldora between 1877 and 1914. It also provides information about the House of Refuge once located 4 miles south of Eldora at what is now Parking Area No. 5. Houses of Refuge were established on the Florida coast to provide shelter for shipwrecked travelers.

The vanished town of Eldora is typical of many small villages along Florida's coast in the 1800s. For a time it thrived with scores of people—perhaps as many as 200—who made their living as carpenters, fishermen, beekeepers, and farmers. Shallow draft steamboats would stop and take on such goods as honey and saw palmetto berries. The palmetto berries were used for pharmaceutical purposes, as they still are today.

Once Harry Flagler built his railroad on the mainland, trains proved to be much cheaper for transportation than steamboats and Eldora turned into a resort for wealthy winter vacationers. The population continued to decline and in 1975, when the NPS took over the property, only about ten persons still lived here. Most were fishermen. You can use the dock in front of the State House for fishing in the Indian River.

In back of the house on the right side is a boardwalk that offers a different return walk, taking you through the heart of a coastal forest. This sometimes is a good spot for birding early in the morning. Beware of mosquitoes.

Miles and Directions

0.0 Start trail at kiosk and enter thick hammock on wide sandy path.

0.13 Arrive at fishing pier. Turn left onto paved trail.

0.25 Arrive at Eldora State House.

0.27 To the right of the State House, arrive at boardwalk that enters thick hammock.

0.38 Walk ends with return to Parking Area No. 8.

Eldora Hammock Trail

Finding the trailhead: Follow A1A about 1.9 miles from the seashore entrance to where the road makes a Y. Go right for 0.2 mile to Parking Area No. 9, site of the trailhead. This is just around the corner from Parking Area No. 8 (Eldora Trail). **GPS:** N28 54.561' W080 49.113'

The Hike

This 0.25-mile loop trail goes through a thick coastal forest where mosquitoes can be fierce and the infrequently used trail is clogged in many places by the webs of banana spiders. The large speckled spiders are harmless, but their webs are very annoying. This sometimes is a good spot for birding early in the morning.

Miles and Directions

0.0 Start from parking lot.

0.03 Pass two large oaks on the right side of the trail.

0.04 Trail makes a sharp right.

0.11 Pass several large cut logs.

0.23 Turn left to return to parking lot.

0.25 Arrive at parking lot.

Castle Windy Trail

Finding the trailhead: The southernmost walk at Apollo Beach begins at Parking Area No. 3 on A1A. The trail starts opposite Parking Area No. 3 on the Indian River side of A1A. **GPS:** N28 53.895' W080 48.218'

The Hike

This short (0.6-mile), straight trail crosses from the beach to Mosquito Lagoon, a part of the Indian River ranked as one of Florida's best fishing areas. An interpretive brochure available from the north end visitor center explains the coastal vegetation and how it has adapted to wind and salt spray coming off the Atlantic.

In a relatively short space, this trail has more than a dozen different ID stops demonstrating how plants are divided into distinct zones based on soil, moisture, and exposure to the ocean. The live oak trees here, for instance, are pruned by salt-laden winds that kill the bud ends and restrict the trees' upward growth. Going farther inland, this effect is lessened and trees are able to grow taller.

At the end of the walk you'll reach an Indian midden (shell mound) near the shore of the Indian River. Like the one at Turtle Mound, it was built by the Timucuans. Called Castle Windy, shells and other objects from it have been dated to 1,000 A.D. Castle Windy's midden is largely unprotected. No climbing or souvenirs-taking permitted.

Miles and Directions

0.0 Cross A1A and join marked trail. Go straight.

0.14 Pass bench on the left. Continue straight.

0.30 Reach shell mound. Go straight.

0.32 Reach shore of Mosquito Lagoon and the Indian River. Small cleared area with one picnic table. End of hike. Retrace your steps.

0.64 Arrive back at Parking Area No. 3.

More Information

Local Information

City of New Smyrna Beach: www.cityofnsb.com.
Southeast Volusia Chamber of Commerce: www.sevchamber.com.

Local Events/Attractions

Want to visit yet another Indian mound? You'll have to drive back to the mainland to find Seminole Rest, just east of U.S. Highway 1, north of Oak Hill. Exhibits along the 0.5-mile trail lead to an 18-foot mound that dates back to 4,000 years ago and was used until about 500 years ago. In the early 1900s, it was common to use shell mounds like these for road fill, but local residents refused to sell this particular mound, preserving an important part of history.

Lifeguards are on duty at Canaveral National Seashore from Memorial Day through Labor Day. Turtle Watches are available June and July. Park visitors can join a ranger and watch a loggerhead sea turtle nest on the beach. Reservations are taken in May for June programs and June for July programs. Call (321) 867-4077 or (386) 428-3384, ext. 10. Fishing piers are located at Parking Area Nos. 7 and 8 in the North District.

Lodging

Southeast Volusia Chamber of Commerce: www.sevchamber.com.

Camping

Two backpacking sites are available along a canoe trail in the northern section. Beach camping is permitted in some areas except from April 1 to November 1 due to sea turtle nesting.

Organizations

National Park Service: www.nps.gov.
Friends of Canaveral: Canaveral National Seashore, 308 Julia Street, Titusville, FL 32796.

Driving the short distance to Canaveral National Seashore's different trailheads, any time you see a boardwalk leading towards the water you should make that brief walk. You might find a scene as lovely as this view of the Indian River.

2 Merritt Island National Wildlife Refuge: Wildlife and Nature Trails

Alligators are a common sight in many places on the Merritt Island NWR.

Created from excess National Aeronautics and Space Administration (NASA) land during the development of the U.S. space exploration program, the 140,000-acre Merritt Island Refuge is Central Florida's principal wildlife habitat. Essentially, it is a huge expanse of chest-high salt marsh grass (with accompanying mosquitoes; carry mosquito repellent at all times) punctuated by small ponds and hammocks, and mosquito control dikes dating from the 1950s. The Cruickshank Trail, featured below, leads to some of the prime bird habitat. Over 500 species of wildlife inhabit the refuge, with 15 listed as federally threatened or endangered. In addition, the refuge contains several wading bird rookeries, 2,500 Florida scrub jays, 10 active bald eagle nests, and numerous osprey nests. During spring months, several hundred manatees may swim in the nearby Indian River.

Start: Either off State Road 406 or State Road 402, depending on hike
Distance: The longest walk is 5 miles; the shortest is 0.7 mile.

Approximate hiking time: 3 to 4 hours, all hikes
Difficulty: Easy to moderate
Trail surface: Natural path

Seasons: Fall through spring; best in winter
Other trail users: Birders
Canine compatibility: No pets
Land status: National wildlife refuge
Nearest town: Titusville
Fees and permits: None for day hiking
Schedule: Hiking trail open daylight hours; Visitor Information Center open weekdays 8:00 a.m. to 4:30 p.m.; Saturday 9:00 a.m. to 5:00 p.m. Sunday hours vary by season. For waterfowl hunting season, visit www.fws.gov/merrittisland/waterfowlhunting/index.html.
Maps: None needed. Refuge overview map available at www.fws.gov/merrittisland/publications/MINWRmap00.pdf
Trail contacts: Merritt Island National Wildlife Refuge, P.O. Box 6504, Titusville, FL 32782; (321) 861-0667 or www.fws.gov/merrittisland. The Visitor Information Center is 5 miles east of U.S. Highway 1 in Titusville on SR 402.

MIGRATING WATERFOWL

From early fall through winter, migrating waterfowl appear at Merritt Island NWR in truly staggering numbers. As many as 310 species of birds have been recorded, and a good winter bird count goes something like this: 50,000 to 70,000 ducks; 100,000 coots; 12,000 to 14,000 gulls and terns; 2,000 raptors, and enormous numbers of songbirds. The only other Florida site that supports a bird population anywhere near this size is Lake Okeechobee to the south, and it is considered second-best.

Besides the huge waterfowl migration, spectacular migrations of passerine birds, such as warblers, occur in spring and fall. Eight species of herons and egrets are commonly in residence. Nesting populations of bald eagles, brown pelicans, mottled ducks, and wood storks are a special feature at the refuge. If you're seriously interested in birding, be sure to obtain a copy of the bird checklist available at the visitor center. Prime birding times are always early and late in the day. Binoculars and a powerful telephoto lens enhance the experience tremendously. Best months for observing birds are November to March.

Allan Cruickshank Memorial Trail

Finding the trailhead: From Interstate 95 just north of Titusville, take exit 220 toward State Road 46. Drive east for 0.3 mile and turn right onto SR 406 (also called Max Brewer Memorial Highway). Follow SR 406 to Black Point Wildlife Drive. Turn left onto Black Point Wildlife Drive and travel about midway, or 3.4 miles, to the parking lot at Stop 8. The Cruickshank Trail begins here. **GPS:** N28 40.691' W080 46.310'

The Hike

This 5-mile loop path is named for wildlife photographer and naturalist Allan D. Cruickshank, who was instrumental in the establishment of the refuge. The walk takes

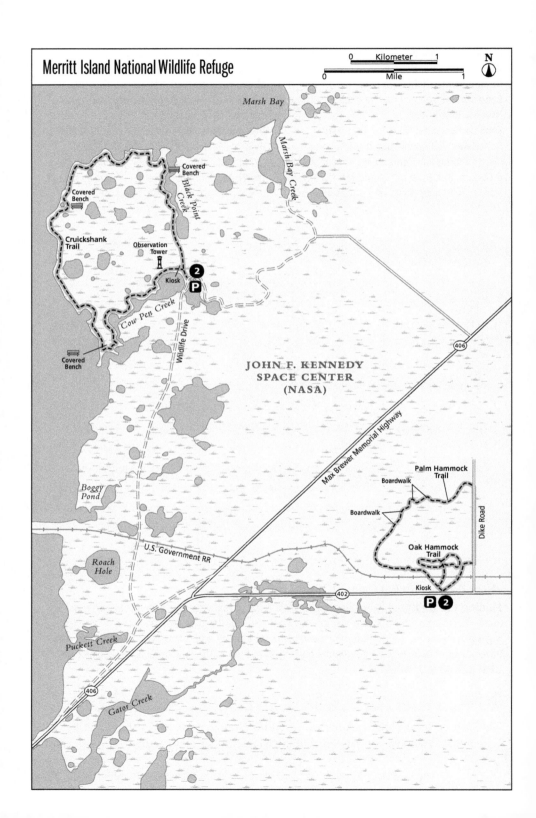

Merritt Island National Wildlife Refuge

Kilometer

Mile

N

Marsh Bay

Marsh Bay Creek

Covered Bench

Black Point Creek

Covered Bench

Cruickshank Trail

Observation Tower

Kiosk

2
P

Covered Bench

Cow Pen Creek

Wildlife Drive

JOHN F. KENNEDY
SPACE CENTER
(NASA)

406

Max Brewer Memorial Highway

Palm Hammock Trail

Boardwalk

Boardwalk

Dike Road

Oak Hammock Trail

Kiosk

P **2**

Boggy Pond

U.S. Government RR

Roach Hole

402

Puckett Creek

406

Gator Creek

between two and three hours. The hike circles a shallow-water marsh that provides excellent birding. An observation platform and a photography blind, visible from the parking lot, are located just a short way along the trail. If it's the right time of day, you might want to climb the platform now for photography. Otherwise, leave it for the end of the walk, as both a good place to rest and to see what else there might be to photograph.

The trail starts as a jeep road and then becomes a little rougher. The walk is somewhat similar to the wildlife drive—a path bordered by open water and man-groves—but with much less traffic. The best time for hiking in what is considered one of Florida's premier birding areas is early morning or mid-afternoon, when the birds are usually most active. You'll probably see alligators in drainage ditches along the trail (you should be perfectly safe as long as you don't provoke them) and wading birds such as blue herons, shorebirds, and waterfowl.

▶ Merritt Island NWR contains more endangered species than any other refuge in the continental United States.

The impressive bird list identifies 310 species sighted in the refuge over the years. Besides the huge waterfowl migration, spectacular migrations of passerine birds, such as warblers, occur in spring and fall. Eight species of herons and egrets are commonly in residence. Nesting populations of bald eagles, brown pelicans, mottled ducks, and wood storks are a special feature at the refuge. If you're seriously interested in birding, be sure to obtain a copy of the bird checklist available at the visitor center. The best months for observing the profuse bird life are November to March.

During November or December, visitors may be surprised to hear the sounds of shotguns adjacent to the wildlife drives. Duck hunting has been an annual ritual here for generations and is still permitted, but only on a tightly controlled quota basis. The hunting is an important aspect of waterfowl management.

Miles and Directions

0.0 Start at the parking lot at Stop 8 on Black Point Wildlife Drive.

0.6 Pass the old boardwalk to a photographer's blind.

0.8 Pass a shaded bench.

1.4 Enjoy a panoramic view of the lagoon.

2.0 Reach Marker 3.

2.2 Pass a bench and a good view of NASA's Vehicle Assembly Building, where spacecraft are prepped for flight.

3.0 Reach Marker 2.

3.7 Pass a covered bench.

4.7 Reach the observation tower.

5.0 Arrive back at the parking lot.

Palm Hammock Trail

Finding the trailhead: From Interstate 95 just north of Titusville, take exit 220 toward State Road 46. Drive east for 0.3 mile and turn right onto SR 406 (also called Max Brewer Memorial Highway). Follow SR406 for 2.8 miles. Turn right onto SR 402 (Playalinda Beach Road). Go straight for 1.7 miles to reach the Visitor Information Center. The common trailhead for Palm and Oak Hammocks is less than another mile farther east beyond the visitor center. The two trails begin from the small parking lot on the left. The different trailheads are clearly marked. **GPS:** N28 38.645' W080 42.996'

The Hike

The 2-mile Palm Hammock loop trail is the longer walk that bears left from the common trailhead. The trail is usually muddy and wet following rains. A sign at the start of the trail indicates whether conditions are "wet" or "dry." In very wet periods the trail may be rerouted, which will be noted on the sign. Several boardwalks span the wettest sections. The trail passes through cabbage palm hammocks, hardwood forest, and open marsh. Don't forget the bug spray.

Miles and Directions

0.0 Leave from the parking lot on SR 402, bearing left.

0.1 Trail veers further left to go into a dense hammock.

0.6 Reach boardwalk with bench on left.

1.2 Pass NASA instrumentation.

1.4 Trail turns right.

1.8 Bridge crosses swamp area.

2.0 Arrive back at parking lot.

Oak Hammock Trail

Finding the trailhead: This 0.7-mile loop trail shares a common trailhead (and parking lot) with the Palm Hammock Trail (above). **GPS:** N28 38.645' W080 42.996'

The Hike

This thirty-minute walk winds through a subtropical forest. The dense, bright green fern bed at the start of the hike is one of the more colorful parts of the plant community, explained in a series of interpretive signs. In addition to large oak trees, you'll pass through a grove of citrus trees. Indian River oranges and grapefruit are nationally famous, first planted in the area around 1830. This particular grove dates from the 1940s.

Miles and Directions

0.0 Leave from the parking lot on SR 402, bearing right.

0.5 Turn left at boardwalk.

0.7 Arrive back at parking lot.

More Information

Local Information
Titusville Area Visitors Council: www.spacecityflusa.com.

Local Events/Attractions
Fishing is allowed on the refuge throughout the year in the scattered pockets of fresh water found on the property. For saltwater angling, wading the shoreline for redfish and trout can be extremely productive in spring.

Canaveral National Seashore, adjoining the refuge, has 25 miles of unbroken beach. One of the best, Playalinda, is quite close to this trail. Call (321) 867-4077, or visit www.nps.gov/cana.

The Kennedy Space Center offers public tours and shuttle launch schedules: www.nasa.gov/centers/kennedy/home/index.html.

Lodging
Lodging is available in Titusville. **Titusville Area Visitors Council:** www.spacecityflusa.com.

Camping
There is no camping within the refuge. For nearby campgrounds, log on to www.spacecityflusa.com.

Organizations
U.S. Fish & Wildlife Service, southeast region: www.fws.gov/southeast.
Merritt Island Wildlife Association: www.nbbd.com/npr/miwa.

3 Honeymoon Island State Park: Loop Trail

Look for nesting ospreys, the fish hawk with the distinctive brown band across its eye, along Honeymoon Island's Osprey Trail.

With miles of white sand beach, this island has 3 miles of trails worth exploring, especially if the weather is acting up and the boat ride to Caladesi looks too rough. The island contains more than 200 species of plants in its mangrove swamps, sea grass beds, salt marshes, tidal flats, and sand dunes. It also contains one of the few remaining virgin, uncut stands of South Florida slash pine.

Nearest town: Dunedin
Start: Northern end of the park's parking lot
Distance: Approximately 3 miles of nature trails
Approximate hiking time: 1.5 to 2 hours
Difficulty: Easy
Trail surface: Natural
Seasons: Anytime
Other trail users: Nature lovers, pet owners
Canine compatibility: Dogs are allowed at the pet beach on the island's southern tip and on the nature trail; they must be on a 6-foot hand-held leash
Land status: State park
Fees and permits: $5 per vehicle; $3 sunset fee
Schedule: Open daily 8:00 a.m. until sunset
Maps: Available at the park
Trail Contacts: Honeymoon Island State Park, #1 Causeway Boulevard, Dunedin, FL 34698; (727) 469-5942; www.floridastateparks.org/honeymoonisland

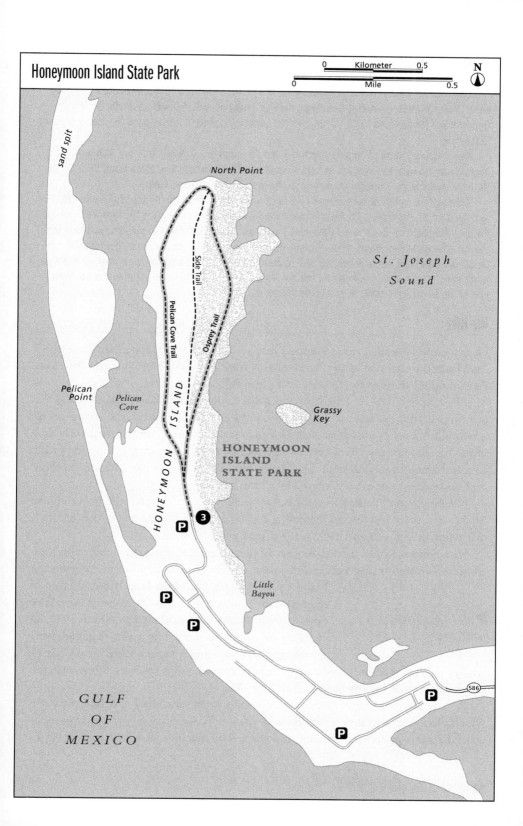

Honeymoon Island State Park

0 — Kilometer — 0.5
0 — Mile — 0.5

N

sand spit

North Point

St. Joseph
Sound

Side Trail

Pelican Cove Trail

Osprey Trail

HONEYMOON ISLAND

Pelican
Point

Pelican
Cove

Grassy
Key

HONEYMOON
ISLAND
STATE PARK

3

P

Little
Bayou

P

P

586

P

P

GULF
OF
MEXICO

Finding the trailhead: Honeymoon Island State Park Area is located at the extreme west end of State Road 586, north of Dunedin.

Coming east from Orlando, take Interstate 4 west to Interstate 275 south to State Road 60 west. Cross Courtney Campbell Causeway, then turn right on U.S. Highway 19 north. Go left on Curlew Road (State Road 586). Follow SR 586, crossing Dunedin Causeway, to Honeymoon Island State Park.

Traveling from north of Tampa, take Interstate 75 south to I-275 south to the Hillsborough Avenue exit. Go west to slight left at Curlew Road (SR 586). Pass fork at State Road 580. Follow SR 586, crossing the Dunedin Causeway, to Honeymoon Island State Park.

Coming from south of Tampa, take I-75 north to I-275 north to the Roosevelt Avenue exit. (Follow signs for St. Petersburg–Clearwater International Airport, last exit before the Howard Franklin Bridge.) Stay right on State Road 686 west when State Road 688 forks to the left. Next turn right (north) onto McMullen Booth Road (County Road 611) to cross over the Bayside Bridge. Go left on Curlew Road (SR 586). Follow SR 586, crossing the Dunedin Causeway, to Honeymoon Island State Park. The common trailhead for the two Honeymoon Island hikes leads from the northern end of the parking lot. **GPS:** N28 04.300' W082 49.936'

The Hike

Honeymoon Island has two connected loop trails that parallel each other. The Osprey Trail leads through one of the last remaining stands of south Florida virgin slash pine. Extending north from the Osprey Trail is the Pelican Cove Trail.

The Osprey Trail is named for the many osprey nests usually found along this coastline. Oyster catchers, snowy plovers, and least terns all nest in the area. Roseate spoonbills, snowy egrets, great blue herons, and many other species frequently feed in the bay and estuaries. Gopher tortoises and armadillos are often seen in the picnic area and along the nature trail. On windy days, Pelican Cove can provide excellent bird observation since it is sheltered by a sand spit.

Ideally, you will make this walk as a loop. Sometimes, however, the Pelican Cove Trail can be quite wet toward the end, and you may want to take one of the side trails that will take you east and back to the drier Osprey Trail.

Honeymoon Island itself is another of those stories about a developer who took an unknown spit of land and tried to make something wonderful of it. Honeymoon Island was previously known as Hog Island because of the hog farm built here in the 1800s. When a New York developer purchased the island for $30,000 in 1939, he changed its name and built fifty palm-thatched bungalows that made the place famous until World War II, when the island became a getaway for tired war production workers. Afterwards, the resort island went into decline.

▶ Good shelling at the north end of the island.

A causeway connecting Honeymoon Island to the mainland was built in 1964, which prompted several more efforts to develop it. Fortunately, in 1970, environmental studies stopped further dredging and filling. The state purchased the land in 1974.

OSPREYS

Often mistaken for the bald eagle, the American osprey is frequently found in its company since the two fish hawks often share the same territory, yet an osprey is only a small shadow of America's national symbol. A more compact bird, it is only 22 to 25 inches in height compared to the bald eagle's more lofty 35 inches. However, its wings are unusually long for its size, extending 55 to 73 inches.

What frequently accounts for the confusion between an osprey and a bald eagle is that both birds are brown and white. However, their color patterns are very different and easy to distinguish.

Where both the head and tail feathers of a bald eagle are an unmistakable white, the upper and tail feathers of the osprey are colored. The osprey has a distinct brown band through its eye and on the side of its face, which easily marks it as different from a bald eagle.

In the Southeast, wherever there is water and fish, the osprey is almost always present. The osprey prefers to nest in the limbs of dead trees, on top of channel markers, or atop telephone or electrical transmission poles. The nests are tall and wide, made of sticks, and reused year after year. Ospreys add to their nests each season, so a long-used nest tends to be huge.

The osprey is one hawk that farmers generally don't mind having on their land, since a nesting pair will usually keep other hawks away. For this reason, some people have erected platforms to encourage the birds to nest in a particular area.

Miles and Directions

0.0 Start at northern end of the parking lot. Go right onto the Osprey Trail.

0.5 Mile marker, keep to the right.

1.0 Kiosk explains osprey's fishing techniques.

1.1 Join Pelican Cove Trail.

1.6 Junction coming from left offers option to rejoin drier Osprey Trail. Assuming conditions are dry enough, continue ahead to stay on Pelican Cove Trail.

1.9 Trail climbs uphill to rejoin Osprey Trail. Go right to return to the parking lot.

2.5 Arrive back at parking lot.

More Information

Local Information

Dunedin Chamber of Commerce: www.dunedin-fl.com.
City of Dunedin: www.dunedingov.com.

Local Events/Attractions

Rental kayaks are available. Fishing for flounder, snook, trout, redfish, snapper, whiting, sheepshead, pompano, Spanish mackerel, cobia, ladyfish, and tarpon. Umbrellas and beach chairs are available for rent.

Sister city to Stirling, Scotland, the Scottish heritage is strong here and the annual Highland Games are a large celebration: www.dunedinhighlandgames.com/games.html.

Lodging

St. Petersburg/Clearwater Area Convention and Visitors' Bureau: www.floridasbeach.com.

Camping

None available in the park.

Organizations

Florida Department of Environmental Protection, Division of Recreation and Parks: www.dep .state.fl.us/parks.

4 Caladesi Island State Park: Beach and Nature Trails

The Beach Trail at Caladesi Island State Park takes you to one of the nation's top beaches.

Located 3 miles offshore in the Gulf of Mexico, Caladesi Island is one of Florida's largest undeveloped barrier islands. Its magnificent beach has been included on the list of America's Best Beaches six times since 2002, finally ranking as number 1 in the entire nation in 2008. So you know the sands here will be extra fine. Caladesi Island can be reached only by boat, which makes it one of the state's most remote hiking sites. Fortunately, you don't need your own craft to reach it. A scheduled ferry runs frequently from nearby Honeymoon Island State Recreation Area. Those who do have their own boats can overnight at the island's 108-slip marina or anchor offshore. Whether the island ferry runs is based on sea conditions; call ahead during periods of high winds to confirm that it is operating.

Nearest town: Dunedin
Start: On the Caladesi Island dock, at the kiosk
Distance: 3 miles
Approximate hiking time: 1.5 to 2 hours
Difficulty: Easy

Trail surface: Mostly sand, some boardwalk
Seasons: Anytime
Other trail users: Nature watchers
Canine compatibility: Pets are not permitted on the ferry from Honeymoon Island. Pets brought to the island by private boat must be

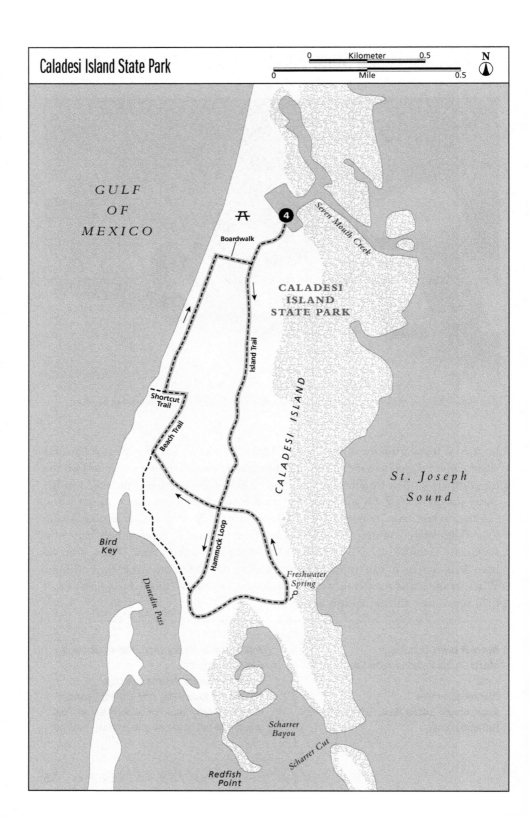

leashed and are not allowed on the beaches, only in a designated area. Pet owners must provide proof of rabies vaccination.

Land status: State park

Fees and permits: Entrance fee under $5

Schedule: Open daily to sunset. The ferry from Honeymoon Island SP to Caladesi Island leaves hourly beginning at 10:00 a.m. The last ferry is 3:00 p.m. To contact the ferry service, call (727) 734-1501.

Maps: Available at entrance

Trail contacts: Caladesi Island State Park, #1 Causeway Boulevard, Dunedin, FL 34698; (727) 469-5918; www.floridastateparks.org/caladesiisland

Finding the trailhead: First, you must take the ferry from Honeymoon Island State Park that departs the west end of State Road 586, north of Dunedin. The ferry leaves hourly beginning at 10:00 a.m.; the last boat is at 3:00 p.m. The hiking trailhead is at the kiosk on the dock where the ferry lands.

Coming east from Orlando, take Interstate 4 west to Interstate 275 south to State Road 60 west. Cross Courtney Campbell Causeway, then turn right onto US Highway 19 north. Go left on Curlew Road (SR 586). Follow SR 586, crossing Dunedin Causeway, to Honeymoon Island State Park.

Traveling from north of Tampa, take Interstate 75 south to I-275 south to the Hillsborough Avenue exit. Go west to slight left at Curlew Road (SR 586). Pass fork at State Road 580. Follow SR 586, crossing the Dunedin Causeway, to Honeymoon Island State Park.

Coming from south of Tampa, take I-75 north to I-275 north to the Roosevelt Avenue exit. (Follow signs for St. Petersburg-Clearwater International Airport, last exit before the Howard Franklin Bridge.) Stay right on State Road 686 west when State Road 688 forks to the left. Next turn right (north) onto McMullen Booth Road (County Road 611) to cross over the Bayside Bridge. Go left on Curlew Road (SR 586). Follow SR 586, crossing the Dunedin Causeway, to Honeymoon Island State Park. **GPS:** N28 01.860' W082 49.222'

The Hike

For 2 miles of gorgeous waterfront walking, follow the boardwalk to the Gulf beach. Long and beautiful, it has been ranked as the best in the entire United States, including Hawaii. Understandably, on summer weekends it becomes crowded, with the rental umbrellas and picnic pavilions offering some of the best beachfront shade.

The boardwalk to the beach also leads to the Island Trail, which in turn connects with two other trail sections to create a 3-mile loop around both the interior and beach. The interior is mostly a closed maritime hammock formed by red bay, sabal palm, live oak, and Southern red cedar. Woodland residents you may encounter include marsh rabbits, armadillos, raccoons, and squirrels.

▶ The island contains many osprey nests, and the excellent beach is ideal for swimming and fishing.

Start the Island Trail by bearing left at the boardwalk and walking straight, meandering first through a scrub forest then passing large salt-tolerant bushes like sea myrtle, a woody plant that can remove salt through its leaves. In fall the plants may be covered with tiny white cloudlike flowers. Another hardy salt-tolerant species along this walk is the sand live oak, a smaller relative to the larger live oak trees so common throughout the state. Leaves of the sand live oak are much more curled, a feature that allows them to survive in a salty, arid environment like Caladesi Island.

Still on the Island Trail, you'll bear right briefly then turn left onto the Hammock Loop, which curves through the island's oldest trees. You are now walking among a stand of Florida's last remaining virgin slash pine. At 1.3 miles on the Hammock Loop, you'll pass a spring of fresh water, the island's largest freshwater source. It is what made it possible for a Swiss immigrant arriving in 1883 to survive on the island for almost fifty years.

The Hammock Loop connects with the longer Beach Trail that skirts the salt marshes and leads down to the beach. Behind the open beach, a dune line populated with sea oats and sea purslane (also called sea pickle) is the favorite nesting area for both sea turtles and birds. Note that the bay side's mangrove swamp attracts numerous shore birds. From the beach, the trail leads back to the access boardwalk that came from the dock.

Miles and Directions

0.0   On the boardwalk leading to the Gulf, go left to join the marked Island Trail.

0.2   Pass anti-litter kiosk. Get interpretive brochure for the three trails. Go straight.

0.6   Ignore Shortcut to the Beach sign. Go straight to see old-growth forest on Hammock Loop.

1.0   Junction with Hammock Loop. Go left.

1.3   Pass freshwater spring on right.

1.8   Hammock Loop ends. Turn right onto Island Trail, then left to join Beach Trail. Continue west.

2.0   Shortcut trail comes in from the right. Ignore; go straight. Prepare for trail to make a sharp left.

2.5   Arrive at first boardwalk going inland and crossing the dunes. Follow boardwalk, go right.

2.8   Junction with Island Trail and access boardwalk coming in from the left. Go left to return to dock.

3.0   Arrive back at ferry dock.

More Information

Local Information
Dunedin Chamber of Commerce: www.dunedin-fl.com.
City of Dunedin: www.dunedingov.com.

Local Events/Attractions
Rental kayaks are available on the island. Fishing for flounder, snook, trout, redfish, snapper, whiting, sheepshead, pompano, Spanish mackerel, cobia, ladyfish, and tarpon. Umbrellas and beach chairs are available for rent.

Sister city to Stirling, Scotland, the Scottish heritage is strong in this region and the annual Highland Games are a large celebration in the nearby city of Dunedin: www.dunedinhighlandgames .com/games.html.

Lodging

St. Petersburg/Clearwater Area Convention and Visitors' Bureau: www.floridasbeach.com.

Camping

No tent camping available in the park. Boaters are allowed to camp overnight on their craft.

Organizations

Florida Department of Environmental Protection, Division of Recreation and Parks: www.dep .state.fl.us/parks.

5 De Leon Springs State Park: Wild Persimmon Trail

Tarzan would probably find more vines to swing from in Central Florida than Africa. Produced by strangler figs, the vines can easily hold the weight of a person.

Although Ponce de Leon probably never tasted the spring waters here, an 1889 advertisement promised visitors that the soda- and sulphur-impregnated waters would act as a veritable fountain of youth. If this were true, you would expect to see a lot of really old people around since the area has been occupied off and on for the past 8,000 years. In fact, one of the oldest canoes ever discovered in the United States, a 6,000-year-old dugout, was found here. A 5-mile section of the Florida Trail loops through a scenic landscape of hammocks, flood plains, and fields. Don't forget to check out the park's famous pancake restaurant before or after your walk.

Nearest town: De Leon Springs
Start: Near the park's interpretive center
Distance: 5-mile loop
Approximate hiking time: 2 to 3 hours
Difficulty: Easy turning to moderate when sections flood during rainy periods
Trail surface: Natural and boardwalks
Seasons: Anytime
Other trail users: Nature lovers
Canine compatibility: Leashed pets allowed

on trail but not around swimming area
Land status: State park
Fees and permits: Admission fee under $5
Schedule: Open 8:00 a.m. to sundown all year
Maps: Included with park admission
Trail contacts: De Leon Springs State Park, 601 Ponce de Leon Boulevard, De Leon Springs, FL 32130; (386) 985-4212; www .floridastateparks.org/deleonsprings

Finding the trailhead: From Interstate 4, take exit 56 and follow State Road 44 to DeLand. At DeLand, drive north from DeLand on U.S. Highway 17 for approximately 6 miles, following the State Park signs. Turn left onto Ponce de Leon Boulevard and go 1 mile to the park entrance. The trail begins behind the bathhouse. **GPS:** N29 08.022' W081 21.682'

The Hike

Laid out and constructed by the Florida Trail Association, this 5-mile walk passes through several types of terrain. Beginning as a paved nature trail with interpretive signs, it moves through an area of bald cypress before the official hiking trail starts. This trail can be rich in wildlife, including deer, turkey, and fox squirrels.

Don't bypass the boardwalk on the left to "Old Methuselah," a huge 150-foot-high bald cypress estimated to be 500 years old. Its girth is 108 inches dbh (diameter at breast height), a standard scale of measurement determined at 4.5 feet off the ground. The pine trees here are equally towering and almost as large around, with some measuring 90 inches or more in diameter. These are truly golden oldies, since pine trees need be only 5 inches dbh to be sold for pulpwood.

▶ A cypress tree estimated to be over 500 years old called "Old Methuselah" is located a short way off the nature trail.

You'll join the orange-blazed Florida Trail section just 0.2 mile from the start as you turn right into a thick, junglelike setting. This very wet jungle provides a boardwalk and a series of bridges to keep your feet dry in most of the perpetually wet areas and to take you across a small stream. Oak hammock, a mix of hardwood and pine, and a cypress dome are all featured along the walk. The trail also crosses an old shell mound left by long-departed Indians who naturally favored the springs for its fresh water and abundance of snails, which were a diet staple. The shell mounds are essentially Amerindian trash piles.

The wild or common persimmon after which the trail is named is at the northern end loop. The persimmon tree, with oval tipped leaves from 3 to 6 inches long, produces a small green fruit that becomes soft, sweet, and orange in color as it matures in the fall. The fruit is a favorite of foxes, skunks, raccoons, opossums, and many bird species. It's normally tart when picked from the tree.

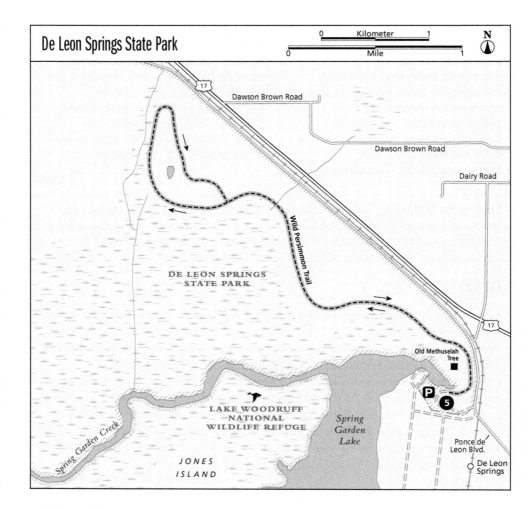

De Leon Springs State Park

0 Kilometer 1

0 Mile 1

N

Dawson Brown Road

Dawson Brown Road

Dairy Road

17

Wild Persimmon Trail

DE LEON SPRINGS STATE PARK

Old Methuselah Tree

17

P

5

LAKE WOODRUFF NATIONAL WILDLIFE REFUGE

Spring Garden Lake

Spring Garden Creek

Ponce de Leon Blvd.

JONES ISLAND

De Leon Springs

Miles and Directions

0.0 Start at the interpretive center nature trail from behind bathhouse.

0.1 Pass short boardwalk to "Old Methuselah," an ancient cypress tree.

0.2 Begin orange-blazed Wild Persimmon Trail.

0.4 Use bridge to cross stream.

0.5 Pass bench. Trail turns more muddy.

0.7 Trail crosses first in series of four boardwalks.

1.0 Cross stream. Continue straight.

1.4 Loop trail return comes in from the right. Go straight (bear left).

1.8 Pass second bench.

2.3 Reach grove of persimmon trees in meadow.

3.5 Trail passes cypress dome.

3.9 Arrive at end of loop trail. Go right to parking lot.

4.0 Re-cross stream.

4.8 Reach end of Wild Persimmon Trail.

5.0 Terminus at interpretive center.

More Information

Local Information

Volusia County Tourism: http://echotourism.com.

Local Events/Attractions

The property has served as a cotton, corn, and sugar plantation known as Spring Garden. The old sugar mill powered by the freshwater spring (19 million gallons daily) has found a new incarnation as part of a grill-your-own pancake house that is extremely popular on weekends. Restaurant hours are Monday through Friday, 9:00 a.m. to 5:00 p.m. and Saturday and Sunday, 8:00 a.m. to 5:00 p.m., serving until 4:00 p.m. Contact: Old Spanish Sugar Mill Post Office, Box 691, De Leon Springs, FL 32130; (386) 985-5644; fax (386) 985-3315; www.planetdeland.com/sugarmill.

Swimming is permitted from 8:00 a.m. until one half hour before sunset. The swimming area is spring fed and is a constant 72 degrees. Depths range from 18 inches to 30 feet at the spring boil.

Canoe rentals are available for exploring Spring Garden Creek, the spring run, which also provides access to 18,000 acres of marshes, creeks, and lakes at the adjacent Lake Woodruff National Wildlife Refuge.

Lodging

Look for lodging at **Volusia County Tourism:** http://echotourism.com.

Camping

None available on site.

Organizations

Florida Department of Environmental Protection, Division of Recreation and Parks: www.dep .state.fl.us.

Friends of De Leon Springs State Park, Inc.: P.O. Box 1444, De Leon Springs, FL 32130.

THE WILY ARMADILLO

Fossil records indicate that armadillos have been around in one form or another for 65 million years, and some of their ancestors weighed several tons.

Armadillos are so unique among mammals that they have been incorrectly named both popularly and scientifically. The name armadillo comes from the Spanish for "little armored one," referring to the armadillo's carapace, or tough shell, something no other mammal wears. However, this outer covering is not at all like the exoskeleton of a tortoise. Instead, the shell is made of modified skin tissue and, despite its imposing appearance, accounts for less than 20 percent of the animal's weight. The average adult is about 2.5 feet long and weighs about fourteen pounds. Males are larger than females.

Armadillos mate anytime between July and December. A single fertilized egg is implanted in the uterus, and four sexually identical embryos develop from this one egg. After a gestation period of at least 150 days, the female bears four identical appearing offspring, which are born with their eyes open. The newborns' shells, initially pliable, begin to harden after a few days. The hardening process isn't completed until the animal reaches its full size.

Caption to come?

6 Lake Woodruff National Wildlife Refuge: Nature Trails

Be sure to check out the observation tower and spotting scope overlooking several pools at Lake Woodruff NWR.

This 21,574-acre refuge offers some of the state's best waterfowl viewing, thanks to a series of dikes that meander around three large lake-size pools. The refuge is a good place for a family outing. The walks vary in length from a 0.5-mile loop walk to the featured hike, a 6-mile round-trip. The banks around the pools are popular for fishing. Local residents often bring folding chairs and ice chests and spend the day.

Blue-wing teals and ring-necked ducks are among the more common winter residents. In spring, wood ducks and their new broods attract much of the attention. The hardwood swamp, freshwater marsh, and pinewoods cater to a large variety of creatures, including black bears, bald eagles, otters, egrets, herons, and alligators.

An observation tower located 0.75 mile from the parking area has a fixed binocular for a good overview of the impoundments and marshes.

Nearest town: De Leon Springs
Start: Refuge parking lot
Distance: Pool 1 to Hontoon Landing, 6.0 miles out and back
Approximate hiking time: 2 to 3 hours
Difficulty: Easy

Trail surface: Dirt path
Seasons: Fall through spring
Other trail users: Fishermen, nature watchers, cyclists
Canine compatibility: Pets prohibited
Land status: National wildlife refuge

Lake Woodruff National Wildlife Refuge

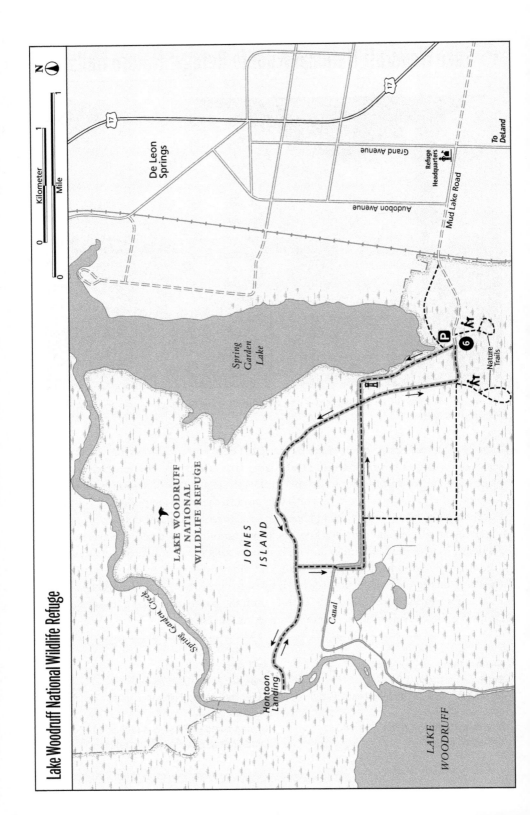

Fees and permits: No fees or permits required for normal day use; hunting permit required in season, September and October
Schedule: Open daily sunrise to sunset
Maps: Available at the refuge office or online at www.fws.gov/lakewoodruff/woodruff_map.html
Trail contact: Lake Woodruff National Wildlife Refuge, 2045 Mud Lake Road, De Leon Springs, FL 32130; (386) 985-4673; www.fws.gov/lakewoodruff; refuge office open weekdays only

Finding the trailhead: The refuge is near DeLand, 25 miles west of Daytona Beach. From DeLand, go north on State Road 17 to De Leon Springs. From SR 17, turn west on Wheeler or Retta Streets to reach Grand Avenue. Go south on Grand Avenue to reach Mud Lake Road. Turn west onto Mud Lake Road. The refuge quarters are on your right. Keep straight (west) on Mud Lake Road. **GPS:** N29 06.402' W081 22.268'

The Hikes

You have several choices of short walks—the open pool trails or shaded nature paths. The pools are within sight of the parking lot. The shortest walk is around Pool 1, a distance of just 1.5 miles. Pools 2 and 3 are considerably larger, a 2.5-mile walk around each. Because the three pools adjoin, it is possible to walk the perimeter of all three pools without retracing your route. The area around Pools 1 and 3 is entirely open (which means it's hot in summer), but the walk atop the earthen dikes is an easy one.

The Live Oak Nature Trail, shortest of the two nature trails, begins at the parking lot. For the longer Oak Hammock Trail, walk straight ahead from the parking lot and along the left-hand side of Pool 1. The trail begins several hundred yards down on the left where Pools 1 and 3 are connected by a common dike.

These nature trails are a vivid contrast to the mostly open pool walks. Both well-shaded trails traverse rich hammocks (the Indian word for shade) of oak and saw palmetto. Portions of the Oak Hammock Trail, however, may get wet after heavy rains. The live oaks common in this region are so named because they bear bright green leaves year-round. The always-green saw palmetto is aptly named for the tiny razor edges along its leaves. Today the berries from the saw palmetto are one of the hottest herbal products on the market. An extract from them is promoted as a preventative against prostate cancer.

In addition to circumnavigating the three pools, it is possible to continue to Hontoon Landing on Jones Island. This add-on segment is quite different from the pool walks—the trail cuts through a forest. The round-trip distance from Pool 1 to Hontoon Landing—without walking all the dikes around the pools—is 6 miles.

Miles and Directions

0.0 Start at the refuge parking lot.
0.75 Reach the observation tower.
3.0 Reach Hontoon Landing, your turnaround point. Retrace your steps.
6.0 Arrive back at the refuge parking lot.

More Information

Local Information
Volusia County: http://echotourism.com (search under "tourism")

Local Events/Attractions
De Leon Springs State Park offers canoeing and hiking trails and a narrated boat tour of the refuge: (386) 837-5537; www.floridastateparks.org/deleonsprings.

Lodging
Lodging is available in the town of DeLand, about 2 miles from the refuge.

Organizations
U.S. Fish & Wildlife Service, Southeast Region: www.fws.gov/southeast/maps/fl.html.

Being able to identify animal tracks and what animals have been on the trail before is a fun learning experience. This is a raccoon track.

7 Hontoon Island State Park: Indian Mound Nature Trail

You'll be lucky to see a river otter out of the water. All you usually see is its splash as it disappears underwater.

Hontoon may not be Robinson Crusoe's island, but in the mushrooming central Florida region, it's the next best thing. Hontoon Island has no land access—visitors arrive by boat. The Park Service provides free ferry service, every fifteen minutes, across the narrow river channel separating the 1,650-acre park from the mainland. Just stand on the dock to attract the boatman's attention. The ferry, which runs from 8:00 a.m. until one hour before sunset, is large enough to carry just people, no cars. The only motorized vehicles on the island belong to park personnel. The island's featured hike, the Indian Mound Nature Trail, leads to a huge Indian shell midden made from tiny snail shells, left by generations of Timucuan Indians, who hunted and fished here for perhaps as long as 3,000 years.

Nearest town: DeLand
Start: Marked trailhead to the right of the dock and behind the administrative offices
Distance: 3.2 miles out and back
Approximate hiking time: 2 hours
Difficulty: Easy
Trail surface: Jeep road, natural surface
Seasons: Fall through spring
Other trail users: Cyclists possibly

Canine compatibility: Pets prohibited
Land status: State park
Fees and permits: Entrance fee under $5
Schedule: Open 8:00 a.m. until sunset
Maps: Available at the park office
Trail contact: Hontoon Island State Park, 2309 River Ridge Road, DeLand 32720; (386) 736-5309; www.floridastateparks.org/hontoonisland

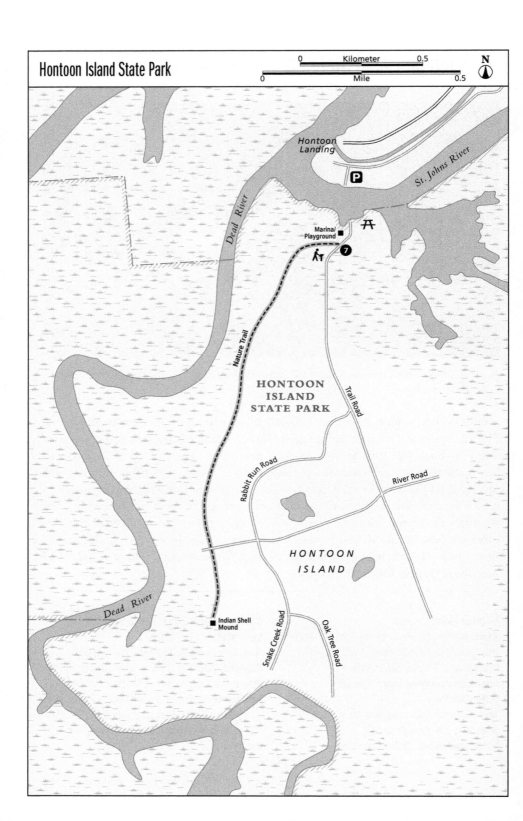

Finding the trailhead: Take U.S. Highway 17/92 to DeLand from Interstate 4. Turn left onto State Road 17. Stay on SR 17 for several miles before turning left onto State Road 44. Go west. Turn left onto County Road 4110 (Old New York Avenue). Follow CR 4110 to County Road 4125 (Hontoon Road) and make a left onto River Ridge Road. Continue to the parking area for the park and the ferry launch, on the left. **GPS:** N28 58.474' W081 21.434'

The Hike

First, a sales pitch for Hontoon Island: This is a terrific place for a family weekend. To camp here, visitors must lug their gear to the truck that hauls it to the campsite. Wise campers pack lightly. Or you can avoid the exertion altogether and stay in one of the handful of cottages located near the tent sites. The cottages come virtually complete, except for bedding and food. Plan meals carefully—there are no stores on the island. What you come without, you do without.

Note the large owl totem pole near the dock, a replica of a Timucuan Indian totem pole found in the park. Made from a single tree, the original totem was dredged up in 1955 from deep muck, which had protected it for an estimated 600 years. It was a remarkable find: the only totem pole ever discovered in the entire Southeast. One archaeologist called it the largest wooden effigy ever recovered from a North American archaeological site.

The original is now locked away safely in the Museum of Natural History in Tallahassee. Yet the owl is a main feature at the visitor center of the Timucuan Ecological and Historic Preserve at Fort Caroline National Monument, near the mouth of the St. Johns River east of Jacksonville. One theory is that totems similar to these were used to identify a particular clan. Canoes approaching the island would be able to spot the totem from the water. Two smaller woodcarvings were also discovered: an otter holding a fish and a bird that resembles a pelican.

▶ Hontoon Island State Park offers a Bedtime Story Camper Lending Library of picture books for campers ages four to nine.

The marked trailhead for the Indian Mound Nature Trail begins to the right of the dock and behind the administrative offices. It takes about ninety minutes round-trip, passing first through a slash pine forest and then descending to border Hontoon Dead River and its healthy bald cypress forest for most of the hike.

The trail ends on the bank of Hontoon Dead River, a tributary of the St. Johns. Surrounded by lush growth, the shell mound is immense: 300 feet long, 100 feet wide, and 35 five feet high. Its builders were the Timucuan Indians, who gathered snails from the St. Johns River. The discarded shells accumulated to form large mounds, or middens, on the island

Supposedly used either ceremonially or as a trash heap (depending on whose theory you believe), this mound and others like it probably served another important purpose: During periods of high water caused by hurricanes, they were the highest ground available. Several other shell mounds form small islands in the St. Johns just to the north. Considering the tiny size of the snail shells that compose this mound, it probably took generations to build.

Many mounds like this around the state were destroyed and used for roadbed fill before anyone realized what the mounds really were or had heard of the Timucuan culture.

This trail is an easy walk, but it can be wet in spots after heavy rains.

Miles and Directions

0.0   Start at the Nature Trail sign behind the administrative offices.

1.3   Pass a bench and an opening to a view of the Dead River.

1.6   Arrive at the shell midden. Retrace your steps through the forest.

3.2   Arrive back at the Nature Trail sign.

More Information

Local Information
Volusia County Tourism: http://echotourism.com.

Lodging
Hontoon Island State Park has six very rustic one-room cabins with bunk beds, vinyl-covered mattresses, a ceiling fan, overhead lighting, and one electrical outlet. All cooking must be done outside. Cabins have no bathrooms; restroom facilities are available at a community bathhouse.

Camping
The park has a dozen campsites with good shade, picnic tables, ground grills, and access to a water spigot. Reservations: (800) 326-3521; www.reserveamerica.com/index.jsp.

Organizations
Florida Department of Environmental Protection, Division of Recreation and Parks: www.dep .state.fl.us.

8 Blue Spring State Park: Boardwalk Trail

The boardwalk at Blue Spring State Park near Orlando offers excellent close-up views of manatees in the clear spring run during the winter months.

The West Indian manatee is believed to be the basis of the mermaid legend because of its humanlike face and broad beaverlike tail. Manatees, which may weigh as much as a ton, eat up to a hundred pounds of vegetation every day. They once ranged from North Carolina to Texas, but destruction of their habitat through development and pollution has drastically reduced their population. Only Florida has a resident population of manatees believed to number somewhere around 3,300 animals, which qualifies them for the endangered list.

The manatee, once a four-footed land creature, is a close relative of the elephant. A manatee's front flippers still have vestiges of what would have been nails. Manatees have no natural enemies, although human progress has certainly endangered their chances for survival. The boardwalk at Blue Spring State Park offers a remarkable look at as many as 140 (it keeps increasing!) of the animals in the clear spring water when they flee the neighboring St. Johns River for the warmer 72-degree waters of the spring run each winter. There is nowhere else in the world that offers such a close view of so many manatees in such clear water. The boardwalk borders the entire spring run, with overlooks at several spots. Bring binoculars and a telephoto lens with a polarizer for the best view of Florida's mermaids.

Nearest town: Orange City
Start: Parking lot bordering the St. Johns River
Distance: 1.0 mile out and back
Approximate hiking time: 30 to 60 minutes depending on how many manatees are present
Difficulty: Easy. Wheelchair accessible
Trail surface: Boardwalk
Seasons: December to March, depending on winter temps
Other trail users: The general public, which is fascinated with manatees. School groups are sometimes brought here on weekdays.
Canine compatibility: Leashed pets permitted
Land status: State park
Fees and permits: Entrance fee under $5
Schedule: 8:00 a.m. to sunset
Maps: Available at the park
Trail contact: Blue Spring State Park, 2100 West French Avenue, Orange City, FL 32763; (386) 775-3663; www.floridastateparks.org/bluespring

Finding the trailhead: Coming from the east coast, from Interstate 4 between Orlando and Daytona, take exit 114 and follow the Blue Spring State Park signs. Go south on U.S. Highways 17/92 to Orange City, about 2.5 miles. Turn right onto West French Avenue, which leads to the park entrance on the left. Drive to the main parking lot, which overlooks the St. Johns River. The boardwalk borders the river.

Coming from Orlando, on I-4 take exit 111B toward Orange City. Go 0.4 mile and turn right onto Enterprise Road. Drive for 0.9 mile and turn right onto South Volusia Avenue, which turns into North Volusia Avenue in 1.7 miles. Proceed straight on North Volusia for another 0.2 mile, then turn left onto West French Avenue, which leads to the park entrance on the left. Drive to the main parking lot, which overlooks the St. Johns River. The boardwalk borders the river. **GPS:** N28 56.569' W081 20.469'

The Hike

This 0.5-mile walk borders the edges of the clear spring run. Wheelchair accessible, the boardwalk has several platforms overlooking the water to provide excellent views of the manatees that winter in the constant 72-degree spring run, which empties into the St. Johns River.

As mammals, manatees are susceptible to cold and need to spend the winters in refuges like this. Once the St. Johns River warms up, the manatee herd disperses until the following November or December. There is no vegetation growing in the spring run, so manatees have to make frequent, short forays into the cold St. Johns River for food.

The best time to see manatees is early in the morning, shortly after the park opens, when a hundred or more animals rest on the bottom, rising to the surface to loudly inhale breaths of fresh air.

And make it a weekday, unless you are there as soon as the park opens at 8:00 a.m. Manatees are

▶ Blue Spring offers scuba-diving in its crystal-clear, 72-degree spring run. Divers must register at the entrance station and have an up-to-date certification card and a partner. Diving with manatees is not permitted. Special weekend manatee programs are offered during manatee season.

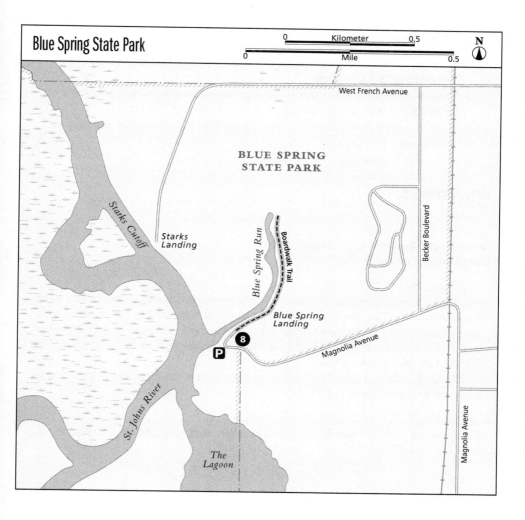

0 Kilometer 0.5
0 Mile 0.5

N

West French Avenue

BLUE SPRING
STATE PARK

Starks Cutoff

Starks
Landing

Blue Spring Run

Boardwalk Trail

Becker Boulevard

Blue Spring
Landing

8

P

Magnolia Avenue

St. Johns River

Magnolia Avenue

The
Lagoon

an extremely popular attraction, and the park often fills on winter weekends. Cars line up and wait until parking spaces empty again. Even weekdays can be crowded, with busloads of schoolchildren, but they typically do not arrive before 10:00 a.m.

The boardwalk also passes through a heavily wooded hammock and ends at the boil of Blue Spring. Fish life in the immediate vicinity of the boil is scarce, due to the water's low oxygen content. However, it can become quite abundant just a few hundred feet down the run—particularly garfish and big tilapia.

Returning, you may be more interested in the large white house on the left, the Thursby House, one of the original plantation houses on the St. Johns and dating from 1872. The Thursbys are considered the area's first pioneer settlers after the British departed.

Miles and Directions

0.0 Start from parking lot closest to St. Johns River. Go straight and to the right to join the boardwalk bordering the spring.

0.2 Overlook of spring run on left. Concession stores and manatee presentations are in the small complex of buildings on the right.

0.5 Arrive at overlook of Blue Spring boil. It is possible to swim/dive here when manatees are not present.

1.0 Arrive back at parking lot.

More Information

Local Information

Volusia County Tourism: http://echotourism.com.

Orange City: www.ci.orange-city.fl.us.

Local Events/Attractions

Rental canoes are available, and a narrated scenic boat tour departs once in the morning and in the early afternoon. A manatee festival is held in Orange City every January. Outside of the winter manatee season, a two-hour narrated nature and ecological cruise is offered on the St. Johns River with a Florida naturalist. In addition to the normal park entrance fee, the boat cruise is $20 for adults, $14 for children three to twelve.

Blue Spring State Park also offers the Bedtime Story Camper Lending Library of picture books for campers aged four to nine.

Lodging

Six cabins in the park each have two bedrooms, heat, air-conditioning, and a full kitchen. No pets are allowed in the cabins.

Camping

The park has fifty-one developed campsites and the four primitive sites that require a 4-mile walk. Reservations: (800) 326-3521 or www.reserveamerica.com/index.jsp.

Organizations

Florida Department of Environmental Protection, Division of Recreation and Parks: www.dep .state.fl.us.

9 Tibet-Butler Preserve: Nature and Perimeter Trails

The long boardwalk at the Tibet-Butler Preserve leads through a large stand of cypress trees.

Anyone visiting the nearby theme parks should spend several (fee-free!) hours walking this self-guided interpretive nature trail and visiting its educational environmental center with (fee-free!) exhibits. The Tibet-Butler Preserve is a rare chance to see real nature in the midst of the world's theme park capital; did we mention it was fee-free? Virtually surrounded by huge theme parks and housing developments, the 440-acre Tibet-Butler Preserve is one of the few "real" things left on the west side of Orlando. The preserve is located on the northeast side of Lake Tibet-Butler, part of the Butler Chain of Lakes.

In addition to several miles of hiking trails, the park also contains the Vera Carter Environmental Center, which offers an excellent interpretation of the plants and animals found on the preserve. Of particular note is the frog exhibit that allows you to re-create the night sounds made by several different species including the remarkable "pig frog." Yes, it does indeed sound like a pig, and you're likely to hear its call at dusk near the marshes.

Nearest town: Windermere
Start: Behind the Vera Carter Environmental Center
Distance: Series of short trails that can be linked for a 4-mile walk
Approximate hiking time: A leisurely 2 hours
Difficulty: Easy
Trail surface: Mix of natural and paved trails
Seasons: Fall through spring
Other trail users: Walking paths only
Canine compatibility: Pets not permitted

Land status: County park
Fees and permits: None needed; free admission
Schedule: Open 8:00 a.m. to 6:00 p.m. Wednesday through Sunday; closed Monday and Tuesday
Maps: Available at the Environmental Center
Trail contacts: Tibet-Butler Preserve, 8777 County Road 535, Orlando, FL 32836; (407) 876-6696; www.orangecountyfl.net/dept/cesrvcs/parks/ParkDetails.asp?ParkID=39

Finding the trailhead: From Interstate 4, take exit 68 at Lake Buena Vista and go north past the shopping centers onto County Road 535 (also the Winter Garden–Vineland Road). The preserve is 5 miles ahead, on the right. **GPS:** N28 26.563' W081. 32.476'

The Hike

Obtain a trail guide from inside the environmental center. At the rear of the center, turn right to join the self-guided Pine Circle interpretive. The walk follows an old fire plow line used to fight a wildfire here in the late 1980s. The trail goes through pine flatwoods and oak hammocks, past longleaf pine and saw palmetto.

Near its end Pine Circle joins the Fallen Log Crossing Trail to penetrate deeper into the heart of the preserve. Fallen Log Crossing Trail ends when it junctions with Osprey Overlook and the Tarflower Loop Trails. Be sure to explore the Osprey Overlook, which leads to a marsh adjacent to Lake Tibet-Butler. This is a very scenic area with lots of lily pads and cypress trees decorated with long beards of flowing Spanish moss.

From Tarflower Loop you'll retrace your steps a short distance to rejoin Fallen Log Crossing Trail before joining Palmetto Passage, which runs a significant stretch of the preserve's perimeter. Take note of this new trail. Pal-

▶ Look for gopher tortoises in the native plants garden. Bobcat and fox also live on the preserve, but you'd be extremely fortunate to see one.

mettos are notorious for the thick roots they grow near the surface, making them easy to stumble over if you're not paying attention. Palmetto Passage may be wet after rains. Follow Palmetto Passage until you can turn right onto Pine Circle Trail, which takes you to the environmental center and the end of the hike.

The preserve also contains a number of bat boxes, some capable of housing up to 300 bats each. Bats, considered North America's most endangered land mammal, are an important and efficient form of mosquito control. In fact, a single bat can eat up to a quarter pound of mosquitoes every day.

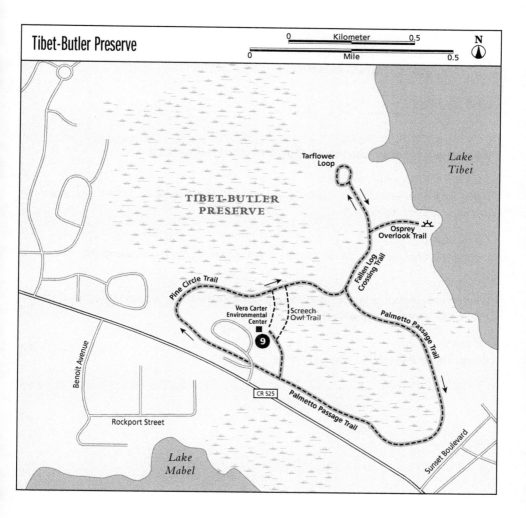

Tibet-Butler Preserve

Kilometer 0 — 0.5
Mile 0 — 0.5

N

Lake Tibet

Tarflower Loop

TIBET-BUTLER PRESERVE

Osprey Overlook Trail

Pine Circle Trail

Fallen Log Crossing Trail

Vera Carter Environmental Center

Screech Owl Trail

9

Palmetto Passage Trail

Benoit Avenue

CR 525

Palmetto Passage Trail

Rockport Street

Sunset Boulevard

Lake Mabel

Miles and Directions

0.0 Start behind Vera Carter Environmental Center. Turn right to reach Pine Circle Trail.

0.2 Reach Pine Circle Trail. Go right.

0.8 Junction with Fallen Log Crossing Trail. Go left to join Fallen Log Crossing. (You also have the option to turn right and return to the environmental center.)

1.2 Junction with Palmetto Passage Trail coming in from the right. Continue straight.

1.5 Fallen Log Crossing junctions with Osprey Overlook Trail as Fallen Log Crossing Trail ends. Take Osprey Overlook Trail and go straight to observation platform on Lake Tibet. Then retrace steps to junction with Fallen Log Crossing Trail. Go right and join the Tarflower Loop.

2.2 Tarflower Loop ends. Retrace steps and go straight to rejoin Fallen Log Crossing.

2.6 Turn left to take Palmetto Passage, a partial perimeter trail.

3.8 Turn right onto Pine Circle Trail.

4.0 Hike ends at environmental center.

More Information

Local Information
Orlando/Orange County Convention & Visitors Bureau: www.Orlandoinfo.com.

Local Events/Attractions
Disney World, Universal Orlando, SeaWorld, and many other attractions are located nearby: www.orlandovacationtravelguide.com.

Lodging
Everything imaginable within a short distance. Check out the options at www.orlandoinfo.com.

Camping
Numerous commercial campgrounds in the area. Unfortunately, the state parks with camping are a good distance away: www.orlandoinfo.com.

Organizations
Orange County Parks: www.orangecountyfl.net.

10 Withlacoochee State Forest: McKethan Lake Nature Trail

Hikers who don't like plastic for water bottles sometimes use novel containers, such as glass Mason jars.

Divided into eight tracts, Florida's third-largest state forest comprises 157,479 acres and spans four counties: Citrus, Pasco, Hernando, and Sumter. Although the World Wildlife Fund has called Withlacoochee "One of the 10 Coolest Places in North America You've Never Seen," about 300,000 people do visit annually. The forest takes its name from the meandering Withlacoochee River, which flows for 13 miles through the forest. From March to November the landscape is often aglow with the brilliant colors of wildflowers. The following hike description covers one of the forest's most popular short walks, the McKethan Lake Nature Trail, a 2-mile loop with numerous interpretive signs. For a longer, multiday hike in the Withlacoochee State Forest, see the 40-mile Citrus Perimeter Loop under "Long Haulers."

Nearest town: Brooksville
Start: McKethan Lake parking area at the kiosk
Distance: 2 miles

Approximate hiking time: 1 hour
Difficulty: Easy
Trail surface: Mixed natural and man-made

Seasons: Fall through spring
Other trail users: Walkers only; no bikes or horses allowed
Canine compatibility: No pets permitted
Land status: State forest
Fees and permits: Daily user fee under $5; permit required for overnight camping, $7 for primitive camping sites
Schedule: Open 8:00 a.m. until sundown; visitor center (located on U.S. Highway 41 about 7 miles north of Brooksville) open 8:00 a.m. to 5:00 p.m. weekdays, 8:00 a.m. to noon and 12:30 to 4:30 p.m. Saturday; closed Sunday
Maps: Available from the Forestry Visitor Center
Trail contact: Withlacoochee State Forest, Recreation/Visitor Center, 15003 Broad Street, Brooksville, FL 34601; (352) 754-6896; www .fl-dof.com/state_forests/withlacoochee.html

Finding the trailhead: From US 41 in Brooksville, go north 7 miles, turn left at McKethan Lake Day Use Area sign. The entrance road is the second paved road north of the intersection of US 41 and Lake Lindsay Road (County Road 476). The trailhead is on the right at the end of the paved one-way road that circles around the lake.

From the intersection of State Road 44 and US 41 in Inverness, go south on US 41 for 12 miles. Turn right at the McKethan Lake Day Use Area sign. The entrance road is the second paved road north of the intersection of US 41 and Lake Lindsay Road (CR 476). The trailhead is on the right at the end of the paved one-way road that circles around the lake. **GPS:** N28 38.674' W082 20.136'

The Hike

The McKethan Lake Nature Trail is a 2-mile nature loop through an unusually diverse forest system. Remarkably, all four species of southern pine (loblolly, sand, slash, and longleaf) grow along the trail. Wildlife includes armadillos (which dig triangular-shaped holes along the trail), possums, raccoons, bobcats, foxes, white-tailed deer, and gray squirrels. Gopher tortoises and golden silk spiders are also quite common.

▶ The state of Florida maintains a herd of longhorn cattle on the nearby Richloam Tract. They are apparently descended from cattle introduced by early Spanish settlers.

The McKethan Lake Nature Trail contains an extensive number of interpretive sites. They include stops at the Devil's Walkingstick, a small tree whose trunk is covered with prickly spines; Tree Sparkle-berry, an understory plant with leathery oval leaves, the bark of which is suitable for tanning leather; and the Resurrection Fern, which alternates from a bright green when moisture is plentiful to a drab brown during drought.

One of the most colorful shrubs is the American beautyberry, which fills with reddish purple berries from August to September. They are a favorite of deer, quail, and most other local wildlife.

Miles and Directions

0.0 Trailhead at parking lot. Walk the trail counterclockwise.
0.2 Enter bottomland hardwood forest. Go straight.
0.7 Bridge crosses McKethan Lake. Continue straight to other side.

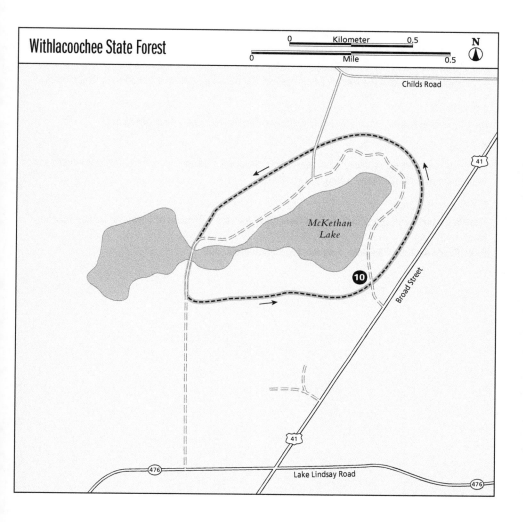

Withlacoochee State Forest

0   Kilometer   0.5
0   Mile   0.5

N

Childs Road

41

McKethan
Lake

Broad Street

10

41

476

Lake Lindsay Road

476

0.9   Enter experimental loblolly pine forest. Continue straight.

1.6   Stand of longleaf pine. Continue straight.

2.0   Trail ends at parking lot.

More Information

Local Information

Citrus County Chamber of Commerce: www.citruscountychamber.com.

Hernando County Chamber of Commerce: www.co.hernando.fl.us/visit.

Pasco County Tourism Development Council: http://visitpasco.net.

Local Events/Attractions

In addition to the described hike, additional trails are available in the 2,500-acre Homosassa Tract and 2,896-acre Two Mile Prairie Tract. The visitor center has maps and directions.

Fishing permitted in the lake; license required. Canoes and boats are limited to trolling motors.

Lodging

Lodging is available in Dade City, Zephyrhills, and Brooksville: http://visitpasco.net.

Camping

Camping is permitted in designated zones only. No open fires are permitted, only cook fires, and even these may be restricted during dry conditions.

Organizations

Florida Department of Agriculture and Consumer Services, Division of Forestry: www.fl-dof.com/state_forests/.

West Pasco Audubon Society: www.westpascoaudubon.com.

Day Hikes

11 Silver River State Park: Sinkhole and Silver River Nature Trails

In Central Florida, most white-tailed deer fawns are born on the edges of open fields or in thickets. They become weaned at about four months.

The short hiking trails at Silver River State Park have been named among America's "Top 15 Hiking Trails" by Reserve America, the organization that handles campground reservations for Florida State Parks and many others. The park is adjacent to Silver Springs, a privately owned attraction whose springhead produces 530 million gallons of water daily to form a huge spring run, in this case the beautiful, clear 7-mile-long Silver River. About 4 miles of the river flow through the 2,300-acre Silver River State Park, an area that would have been rapidly developed in the twentieth century if most of the property weren't lowlands and unsuited for building.

The several short hikes here cover a great variety of terrain, including sinkholes, sandhills, and floodplain forest. Look for several different species of mammals, reptiles, and birds, including armadillos, deer, turkey, fox, Sherman's fox squirrel, and gopher tortoises. Less frequently seen are coyote, bobcats, and black bear. Silver River is the home to a good population of limpkins.

Nearest town: Silver Springs
Start: Hikes begin at the end of the main parking lot
Distance: Four short hikes covering up to 8 miles
Approximate hiking time: 4 to 5 hours for all
Difficulty: Easy
Trail surface: Natural surface, boardwalk
Seasons: Fall to spring
Other trail users: Off-road bikes allowed on most trails
Canine compatibility: Pets are not permitted

in the restrooms, museum, or cabins; they may be taken leashed on the trails and within the campground.
Land status: State park
Fees and permits: Admission fee under $5
Schedule: Open 8:00 a.m. to sunset daily
Maps: Available at the park
Trail contacts: Silver River State Park, 1425 Northeast 58th Avenue (State Road 35), Ocala, FL 34470; (352) 236-7148; www .floridastateparks.org/silverriver

Sinkhole Nature Trail

Finding the trailhead: From Interstate 75, take exit 352 and follow State Road 40 east through Ocala and Silver Springs. At State Road 35, located almost at the corner of the Silver Springs attraction, turn right and go south for 1 mile to the park entrance. Unless the park is full, do not park in the first parking lot but follow the road to the end. An information kiosk with trail maps is on the left. The hike begins from this lot.

From Interstate 95, take exit 268. Drive west on SR 40 toward Ocala and the Silver Springs attraction. At SR 35, located almost at the corner of the Silver Springs attraction, turn left and go south for 1 mile to the park entrance. **GPS:** N29 12.056' W082 02.804'

The Hike

The 2.5-mile loop Sinkhole Nature Trail takes about ninety minutes to walk. Be aware this trail does not go near the river. Soon after you start out, the trail Ts. Go right for the longer walk that will loop you through the woods, across the main park road, and around to a sinkhole with picnic tables. Going left instead will take you to the same sinkhole by a different route and cut your hiking time by two-thirds. But you're here to walk the full length of the trail, attained by going right at the T and following the Sinkhole Trail as it veers left to junction with the 1.7-mile Sandhill Trail loop, which will return you to this same junction if you want to add another forty-five minutes to your hike. The Sandhill Nature Trail can also be accessed from its own trailhead near the park entrance, on the north side of the road. The parking area is well marked.

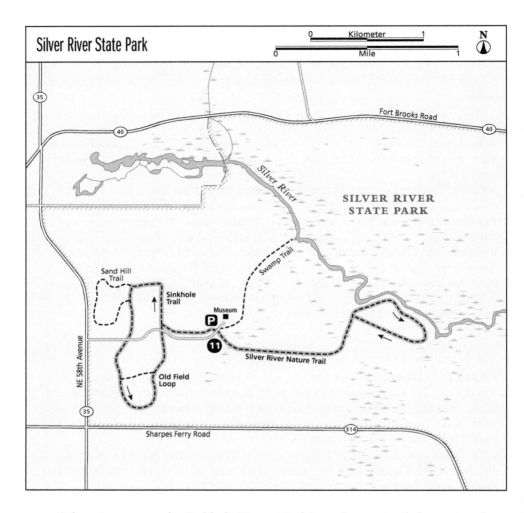

Silver River State Park

Otherwise, stay on the Sinkhole Nature Trail Loop by turning left, crossing the park entrance road, and soon arriving at the sinkhole itself. To enjoy the full 2.5-mile Sinkhole Nature Trail walk, avoid a shortcut side trail coming in from the left. Instead, continue straight to join the Old Field Loop, an interpretive side trail that begins south of the sinkhole.

Miles and Directions

- **0.0** T intersection near the entrance road
- **0.8** Junction with 1.7-mile Sandhill Trail. Go left to stay on Sinkhole Nature Trail.
- **1.1** Cross park entrance road. Trail veers right into dense hammock before continuing south.
- **1.5** Arrive at picnic tables within easy view of the park's largest sinkhole.
- **1.7** Join Old Field Loop by going straight.

2.3 Old Field Loop junctions with Sinkhole Nature Trail.

2.5 Terminus back at parking lot near Cracker Village.

Silver River Nature Trail

Finding the trailhead: At the park's main parking lot, the Silver River Nature Trail starts from the eastern (opposite) end as the Sinkhole Nature Trail. Look for the hiking trail sign. **GPS:** N29 12.061' W082 02.062'

The Hike

The Silver River Nature Trail is 2.1 miles round-trip. It offers not only an excellent view of the waterway river but the chance to experience one of the river's uncommon natural beaches. Once you reach the river, try and spot some of the many small springs populating the bottom that add another 200 million gallons of water daily in addition to the 530 million gushing from massive Silver Springs itself. No wonder the river has such a current.

The Indian name for the Silver River was *Suaille-aha,* meaning "sun glinting water." They considered Silver Spring, the river's water, as sacred; the river itself, because of its purity and beauty, was regarded as a shrine to the water gods. The Silver River extends for 7 miles before running into the Ocklawaha River, largest tributary of the St. Johns River. By 1845 all of the area rivers were used regularly by barges carrying lumber, produce, and cotton. Most of the Native American population had disappeared.

▶ The world-famous glass-bottom boat tours of the Silver River began in the late 1870s when Phillip Morrell fixed a piece of glass in the bottom of a rowboat. The rest is history.

The trail to Silver River is quick and easy, placing you beside the river in just over a half-mile. From the river overlook retrace your steps a short distance and turn left to join the short loop trail bordering the river. This soon leads to another access point to the river on what is essentially a game trail. Continue on the loop through floodplain forest to a man-made observation point with a bench at 1.0 mile. The trail then turns away from the Silver River to rejoin the access main trail at 1.6 miles. Turn left for your return route to the parking lot and a walking distance of 2.1 miles.

Miles and Directions

0.0 Depart from parking lot. At junction with Swamp Trail, go right on Silver River Nature Trail.

0.7 Arrive at open area with view of Silver River. Retrace steps for short distance.

0.73 Turn left onto loop trail bordering Silver River.

1.0 Bench with river view. Continue to the right. Trail will start to loop inland and travel northwest to rejoin main trail.

1.6 Rejoin main river trail. Go left to return to parking lot.

2.1 Return to the parking lot.

More Information

Local Information

Ocala/Marion County Chamber of Commerce: www.ocalacc.com.

Local Events/Attractions

There are two other short walks in the park. The 1.7-mile Sandhill Trail begins just inside the park, on the left, past the ranger station. It winds through sandhill habitat of turkey oak, wiregrass, saw palmetto, and longleaf pine.

The mile-long linear Swamp Trail (2 miles round-trip) ends at a boardwalk overlooking the Silver River. This is strictly a scenic nature walk. Swimming is not possible.

The park's Silver River Museum and Environmental Center is open on Saturday and Sunday from 9:00 a.m. to 5:00 p.m. From June 13 through July 28 the museum may also be open Tuesday through Friday from 10:00 a.m. to 4:00 p.m. There is a fee for all over the age of six. Call (352) 236-5401 for more information. The museum has been named one of the nation's "Top 20 Educational and Historical Facilities" in the annual Reserve America's "Best Outdoor Spots in America."

Lodging

The park offers 10 cabins, each of which sleeps up to 6. Each cabin has a full dining area, two bedrooms, one bath, stove, refrigerator, microwave, dishwasher, gas fireplace, heating and air-conditioning, screened porch, dishes, pots and pans, silverware, linens, towels, picnic tables, and rockers on the porch. They have been recognized twice as among the Top 15 Unique Cabins in the United States by Reserve America, the park's central reservation system at (800) 326-3531; http://ra1.reserveamerica.com.

Camping

The park's Fort King & Sharpes Ferry Camping Areas offer a total of 59 sites able to handle even large RVs. Water and electric hook-ups available with 30 amp service and six sites with 50 amp service. All campsites have fire rings, barbecue grill, and picnic table. A separate dump station is offered for holding tanks. Firewood is available at the ranger station. Reserve at (800) 326-3531; http://ra1.reserveamerica.com.

Organizations

Florida Department of Environmental Protection, Division of Recreation and Parks: www.dep.state.fl.us.

FLORIDA SPRINGS

The world's largest limestone spring is the Silver Springs attraction near Ocala. The spring flow here is tremendous: 530 million gallons of water and more than 430 tons of minerals every twenty-four-hour period. The spring also feeds the 7-mile-long Silver River, actually a spring run. Silver Springs, locale for the pioneering underwater/adventure TV drama *Sea Hunt*, is a commercial operation closed to swimmers; to view its thirty varieties of fish, you have to take one of the glass-bottom boat tours.

Overall, Florida has seventeen of the seventy-five "first magnitude" springs in the United States, more than any other state. A first magnitude spring spews out a whopping 100 cubic feet of water per second. Further, there are another forty-seven springs that rank as second magnitude, which put forth between 10 and 99 cubic feet of water per second. It's an unusual blessing, indeed, to have so many natural swimming pools.

The majority of Florida springs were created this way: underground water (often under a considerable amount of pressure) broke through the ground. The spot where the water emerged is known as the "spring boil." Normally, there is too much water gushing out to be contained in an isolated pool, so rivers or "spring runs" are formed by the overflow. Because all of Florida's springs are fed by the same underground river, the water temperature averages 72 degrees every day of the year, except in the Panhandle, where temperatures average closer to 68 degrees.

12 Bulow Plantation Ruins Historic State Park: Bulow Woods Trail

The Bulow Woods Trail ends near the magnificent Fairchild Oak, an estimated 400 to 500 years old.

A short but striking section of the Florida National Scenic Trail (FNST) encompasses ruins of Florida's largest sugar mill, destroyed in 1836 during the Second Seminole War. Altogether, there were three Seminole Wars in Florida. The Seminoles were never defeated and never signed a peace treaty with the U.S. government. No other Indian tribe can make that claim.

Remains of the plantation include extensive ruins of the sugar mill, a springhouse, and the crumbling foundation of the great house. They are made of coquina (co-KEEN-a), a sedimentary rock found along Florida coasts made mostly of shell fragments and associated with coral reefs. At the sugar mill, interpretive signs explain the process for making syrup from sugarcane. A small building adjacent contains artifacts found on the grounds.

Nearest town: Flagler Beach
Start: Parking lot near park entrance
Distance: 6.8 miles one-way

Approximate hiking time: 3 hours
Difficulty: Easy
Trail surface: Dirt path, unpaved areas

Seasons: Fall through spring

Other trail users: Cyclists in some areas

Canine compatibility: Leashed dogs permitted

Land status: State park

Fees and permits: Park admission fee under $5

Schedule: 9:00 a.m. to 5:00 p.m. Wednesday through Monday; closed Tuesday

Maps: Available at nearby Tomoka State Park (386-676-4050), 4.5 miles south of Bulow Creek State Park on Old Dixie Highway; or the Florida Trail Association (FTA)

Trail contact: Bulow Plantation Ruins Historic State Park, P.O. Box 655, Bunnell, FL 32010; (386) 517-2084; www.floridastateparks.org/bulowplantation

Finding the trailhead: Take exit 268 off Interstate 95 and travel east less than a mile on Old Dixie Highway to County Road 2001, on the left. CR 2001 is also known as Old Kings Road. Go north 2 miles to the brown-and-white state marker at Plantation Road, called Monument Road on some maps. Turn right into Bulow Plantation Ruins Historic State Park. Parking for the hike is on the entrance road before the gate. **GPS:** N29 26.094' W081 08.279'

The Hike

The plantation hike can be done in several ways. The easiest is to drive down Plantation Road, park at the Plantation House site, and walk the quarter mile to the sugar mill ruins. However, it is far more scenic to park at the beginning of Plantation Road and then walk the narrow, beautifully canopied dirt route leading to the ruins.

In addition, you can hike the 6.8-mile Bulow Woods Trail that runs from Bulow Plantation Ruins to Bulow Creek State Park, which contains one of the best stands of live oak on Florida's Atlantic coast. The Bulow Woods Trail crosses open woods before entering the thick canopy of Bulow Hammock. At about the midpoint of the hike you'll see a blue-blazed side trail to what are jokingly called the Cisco Rapids, which is just a small waterfall. Yet even those are rare in Florida. *(Note:* The Florida Trail Association may refer to this same hike as the Bulow Creek Trail. This guide uses the trail name designated by the state park.)

The trail ends at the sprawling Fairchild Oak, one of the older oaks in Florida. Some have estimated its age at an incredible 2,000 years, but it seems to be more in the range of 400 to 500 years.

The once-magnificent Bulow Plantation was built in 1821 by Charles Bulow of Charleston, South Carolina, who also cleared much of the 2,500 acres for sugarcane, cotton, rice, and indigo. Bulow died after only three years of working the estate. The property was taken over by his son John, who fashioned it into one of the finest and wealthiest plantations in Florida. Its sugar mill was one of the largest ever built in the state. Famed wildlife artist John James Audubon visited the estate in 1831 during a painting trip in Florida.

The Seminole Wars ended the prosperous plantation days. Ironically, John Bulow was opposed to the government's plan to send the Seminoles to reservations in the far west. Bulow went as far as firing a four-pound cannon at the state militia when it came on his land.

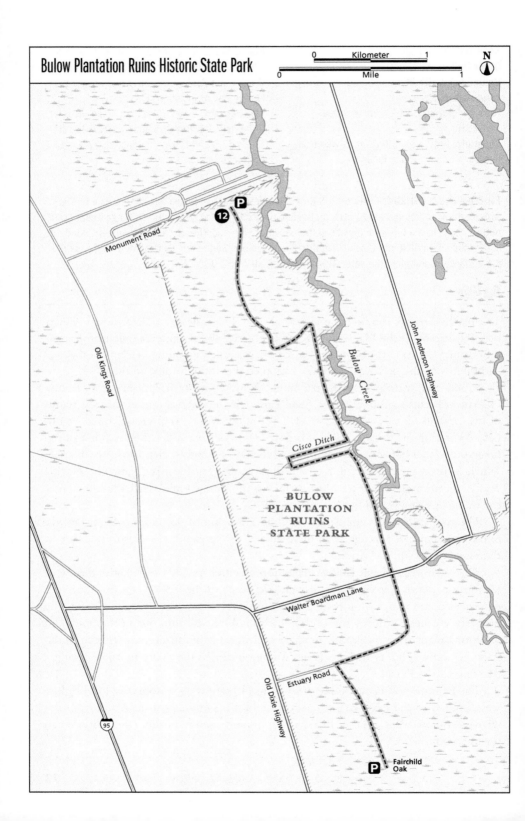

Bulow Plantation Ruins Historic State Park

Still, Bulow realized the Seminoles were becoming increasingly hostile, so he and his slaves abandoned the plantation. It was a wise move. In January, 1836, the Seminoles attacked and burned every plantation built on land the Indians claimed belonged to them. This included Bulow's plantation. Disheartened, Bulow gave up and moved to Paris, where he died before the age of twenty-seven.

Miles and Directions

0.0 Start at the trailhead at parking area before park gate.

0.2 Cross a stream on a footbridge.

0.7 Cross a second bridge.

1.2 Cross yet another bridge.

1.4 Reach a wetter area requiring two bridge crossings.

2.0 Reach Marsh Point.

2.8 The trail follows Cisco Ditch.

3.2 Pass the blue-blazed side trail to Cisco Rapids.

3.8 Cross a power line right-of-way.

4.0 Cross paved Walter Boardman Lane; follow Mound Grove Road.

4.6 Come to the junction with Estuary Road.

4.7 Pass a 0.5-mile blue-blazed side trail to a primitive campsite.

6.8 Arrive at the Fairfield Oak Tree parking area in Bulow Creek State Park. Unless you've arranged for a shuttle or a pickup, retrace your steps.

More Information

Local Information

Ormond Beach Chamber of Commerce: www.ormondchamber.com/obmain.
Daytona Beach Area Convention & Visitors Bureau: www.daytonabeach.com.

Local Events/Attractions

Bulow Creek is a designated State Canoe Trail. Rental canoes are available at the park office.

Daytona and its world-famous raceway are located only a few miles to the south. February is the peak racing month.

Lodging

Lodging is available in Flagler Beach, Ormond Beach, and Daytona Beach.

Camping

Primitive camping is available at nearby Bulow Creek State Park. An overnight permit is required and can be obtained at Tomoka State Park, 4.5 miles south of Bulow Creek State Park on Old Dixie Highway; (386) 676-4050. Reservations: (800) 326-3521; www.reserveamerica.com/index.jsp.

Organizations

Florida Department of Environmental Protection, Division of Recreation and Parks: www.dep.state.fl.us.

The Bulow Plantation ruins show the devastating effects during the Second Seminole War in 1836. This was once the largest plantation in East Florida.

13 Flat Island Preserve: Daubenmire Trail

The snowy egret is one of the area's prettiest birds.

This 2,300-acre preserve located near Leesburg encompasses two wooded islands (Flat Island and Magnolia Island) and a huge wetland known as the Okahumpka Marsh. Of the two islands, Flat Island is the most accessible place for hiking, with three shaded loop trails created and maintained by the Florida Trail Association. Magnolia Island's trails and primitive camping are accessible only by boat via the canal system from the Flat Island Boardwalk. Canoe rentals are available if you decide to venture there. Make advance arrangements with the Lake County Water Authority and download a canoe use permit ahead of time (see "Trail contacts," below).

The Okahumpka Marsh happens to be a uniquely situated marsh, located on the hydrologic divide between surface waters that flow eastward toward the Ocklawaha River and to the Atlantic and westward to the Withlacoochee River and the Gulf of Mexico. Over 110 plant species have been identified in the marsh and on Flat Island. Since this is a marshy area, you can count on mosquitoes except in cooler weather. Bring repellent.

Nearest town: Leesburg
Start: At trailhead off Owens Road
Distance: 3.5 miles
Approximate hiking time: 3 hours
Difficulty: Easy to moderate
Trail surface: Natural surface, boardwalks
Seasons: Fall through spring
Other trail users: Hikers only
Canine compatibility: No pets

Land status: Owned by Lake County Water Authority
Fees and permits: Overnight camping permit needed; available by download (see Trail Contacts, below)
Schedule: Open 8:00 a.m. until sunset daily
Maps: Available online (see Trail Contacts)
Trail contacts: Lake County Water Authority, 107 North Lake Avenue, Tavares, FL (352) 343-3777; www.lcwa.org/index.asp?page=74

Finding the trailhead: From Florida's Turnpike (also the Ronald Reagan Turnpike), leave the toll road at exit 285. Turn onto U.S. Highway 27/Leesburg and State Road 19/Clermont. Go 11.3 miles and turn right onto US 27 to Leesburg. Be prepared to turn left almost immediately onto Connell Road. Go 0.5 mile, turn right onto County Road 25A. Go another 0.5 mile. Turn left onto Owens Road, which leads to the entrance gate almost immediately. **GPS:** N28 46.721' W081 54.168'

The Hike

The trail, open daily from 8:00 a.m. until sunset, is open to foot traffic only. Although Flat Island was farmed and harvested in the past, natural vegetation has reclaimed the island and few traces of earlier development remain. With 110 plant species, some rare and many quite colorful, growing in the area, you'll want to make use of the interpretive signs scattered along the trail explaining the flora and fauna. Of special note is the needle palm, rare in most of Florida but common on Flat Island.

▶ In the early 1900s, Leesburg was an important producer of watermelons and began to hold an annual Watermelon Festival. Times changed, and watermelon growing became so unimportant that festival watermelons have had to be imported from outside the area.

The Main Loop Trail, blazed in orange, makes a 3.5-mile circuit of the island. However, you can shorten the hike to a total of 1.5 miles by taking the Short Loop using the C–D cross trail. The Middle Loop with the E–F cross trail cuts the hike to 2.5 miles. The cross trails are blazed in blue. At the southernmost loop between junction trails C and E is a 440-foot-long boardwalk passing through wetlands that ends at a canoe dock located on the canal to Lake Denham. If you paid the rental and deposit fees at the park caretaker's office back at

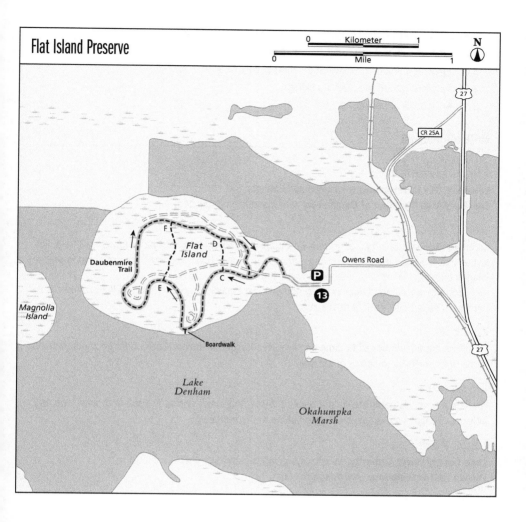

Flat Island Preserve

Kilometer 0 — 1
Mile 0 — 1

N

27
CR 25A
Owens Road
P
13
Daubenmire Trail
Flat Island
F D
C
E
Magnolia Island
Boardwalk
Lake Denham
Okahumpka Marsh
27

the trailhead, you've been carrying paddles and a life jacket so you can take one of these canoes and go exploring in the canal. If birding is a main interest, expect to see many more birds feeding in the marsh canals than walking the Flat Island trail.

Miles and Directions

0.0 Depart from trailhead off Owens Road. Follow the loop clockwise.

0.25 Junction with service road. Go straight.

0.50 Junction with loop road. Go left.

0.65 Junction with first cross trail, C-D, coming from the right. Go straight.

1.1 Junction with 440-foot boardwalk leading to dock and Lake Denham canal.

1.35 Junction with second cross trail, E-F, from the right. Go straight.

1.37 Primitive campsite; water should be treated.

2.35 Junction with second cross trail, F-E, from the right. Go straight.

2.75 Junction with first cross trail, D-C, from the right. Go straight.

3.0 Junction with loop trail. Go left to return to parking area.

3.25 Junction with service road. Go straight.

3.50 Arrive back at parking area.

More Information

Local Information

Leesburg City Government: www.leesburgflorida.gov.

Leesburg Area Chamber of Commerce: www.leesburgchamber.com.

Local Events/Attractions

Venetian Gardens is a 110-acre park with public swimming pool and bath house, ball field, volleyball court, picnic tables, and walking paths around Lake Harris. Pedestrian bridges lead to private islands offering fine views of the lake and the park's canals.

Leesburg is located in appropriately named Lake County. The county's 1,400 lakes make up 17 percent of Lake County's 722,000 acres.

Lodging

Leesburg Area Chamber of Commerce: www.leesburgchamber.com. Look under accommodations in the upper right-hand corner of the site.

Camping

There is a primitive campsite on the back of the far loop trail; permit needed from www.lcwa.org/index.asp?page=74. Camping is also available at the trailhead.

Organizations

Lake County Water Authority: www.lcwa.org/index.asp?page=74.

Florida Trail Association: www.floridatrail.org.

14 Split Oak Forest Mitigation Park: North/Lake and South Loops

Rain occurs frequently in the summer and fall months, but it doesn't stop serious hikers.

This 1,700-acre forest is adjacent to two very picturesque lakes—Lakes Hart and Mary Jane—and also to a very popular county park, Moss Park. The forest is named for a giant 200-year-old oak tree that was split more than fifty years ago but continues to grow today. The forest is owned jointly by Orange and Osceola Counties.

You have two main options for hiking here: the North and South Loop trails. While both include sections of wooded uplands, the South Loop concentrates on a more marshy environment. The North Loop offers more variety, including a side path traversing the lake-fringe habitats of Lake Hart and Bonnett Pond with overlooks of both. The North Loop also provides a connector trail to adjacent Moss Park, which offers camping and usually a large gathering of sandhill cranes in winter.

Some of the wildlife found in Split Oak includes coyotes (rare), alligators, wood storks, red-shouldered hawks, gray foxes, gopher tortoises, and box turtles.

Nearest town: Narcoossee
Start: Kiosk near the main parking area
Distance: North Loop Trail, 3.1-mile loop; Lake Loop, 1.2-mile loop; Swamp Trail, 1.6 miles out and back; South Loop Trail, 4.2-mile loop
Approximate hiking time: 5 to 6 hours for full trail system
Difficulty: Easy to moderate

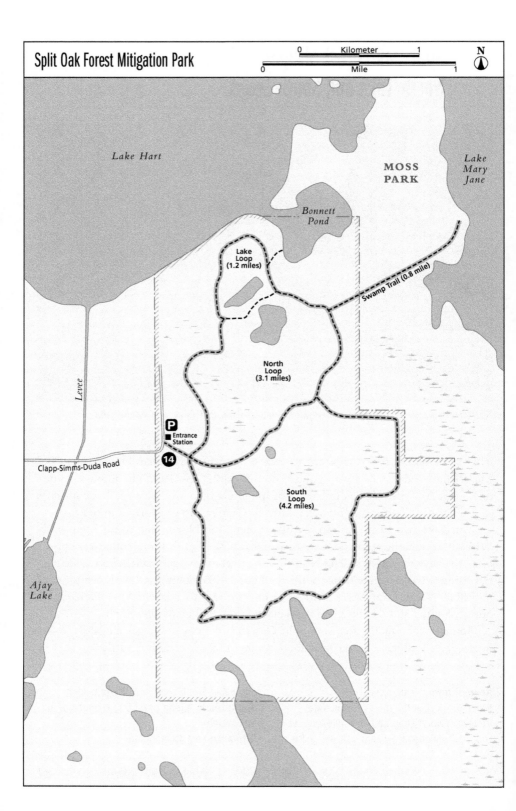

Split Oak Forest Mitigation Park

0   Kilometer   1
0   Mile   1

N

Lake Hart

MOSS PARK

Lake Mary Jane

Bonnett Pond

Lake Loop (1.2 miles)

Swamp Trail (0.8 mile)

North Loop (3.1 miles)

Levee

P
Entrance Station

14

Clapp-Simms-Duda Road

South Loop (4.2 miles)

Ajay Lake

Trail surface: Natural surface
Seasons: Fall through spring
Other trail users: Horses on Saturday only
Canine compatibility: Pets prohibited
Land status: State wildlife management land
Fees and permits: No fees or permits required for day use; license required for freshwater fishing
Schedule: Open sunrise to sunset year-round

Maps: Available at the trailhead
Trail contact: Moss Park, 12901 Moss Park Road, Orlando, FL 32832-6228; (407) 273-2327; www.orangecountyfl.net/dept/cesrvcs/parks/ParkDetails.asp?ParkID=29. Moss Park is located 4 miles southeast of County Road 15 (Narcoossee Road) on Moss Park Road.
Special considerations: Bicycles and firearms prohibited

Finding the trailhead: Split Oak Forest is located in Orange and Osceola Counties, approximately 16 miles south of Orlando. From Orlando International Airport, go east on State Road 528 (Beeline Expressway) for 2.5 miles to exit 13. Go south on County Road 15 (Narcoossee Road) for 7 miles. Turn east onto Clapp-Simms-Duda Road and follow signs to the entrance. **GPS:** N28 21.200' W081 12.655'

The Hikes

North & Lake Loop Trails

The 3.1-mile North Loop Trail is blazed in green. It includes all three lakes and the split oak for which the forest is named. The North Loop also provides access to Moss Park on a blue-blazed connector trail, although this trail may be underwater during the rainy season. The North Loop shares the South Loop path at the beginning. Therefore, it is especially important to pay attention to the blaze colors when the trails separate. When trails overlap, both blaze colors are used. Just make sure you continue to follow the correct color when the trails split.

▶ One of the purposes of Split Oak Forest is to protect and preserve the habitat of the gopher tortoise, a state and federally listed species.

The 1.2-mile Lake Loop, blazed in blue, is an extension of the North Trail and can only be reached from it. The habitat here is classic to central Florida and includes cypress swamps, pine flatwoods, oak hammocks, and marshland. Three lakes on the property, one of them quite close to the trailhead, are open to fishing. The most common residents are sandhill cranes, wood ducks, owls, wood storks, eagles, bobcats, white-tailed deer, gopher tortoises, and pileated woodpeckers.

Miles and Directions

0.0   Start at parking lot kiosk. Follow the common trail marked with green and yellow blazes.
0.4   The North and South Loop Trails split; go left to stay on the green-blazed North Loop.
1.4   The trail intersects the blue-blazed Lake Loop. Turn left to join the Lake Loop.
2.1   Side trail on the left to platform overlooking Bonnett Pond.

2.3 End of Lake Loop rejoins the green-blazed North Trail. This is also the site of the great split oak for which the park is named. Continue by bearing left on the North Trail.

2.6 The 0.8-mile Swamp Trail leading to Moss Park comes in from the left. Stay on North Loop.

3.2 Reach the junction of North and South Loop Trails. From here it is 1 mile back to the parking lot, combining the 0.6-mile cross trail with the 0.4-mile access trail. If you continue on the South Loop, the total hiking distance back to the parking lot is 6.7 miles.

3.8 Reach junction with western end of North Loop. Go straight to return to parking lot.

4.2 Arrive back at parking lot.

Swamp Trail

The 1.6-mile out-and-back Swamp Trail, the shortest trail in the forest, is also an extension of the North Loop Trail that leads to Moss Park.

South Loop Trail

The 4.2-mile South Loop Trail, blazed in yellow, shares the North Loop path at the beginning. Pay attention to the blaze colors when the trails separate to make sure you follow the correct color when the trails split. The South Trail typically is the least used but has some of the best wildlife viewing, especially for sandhill cranes (the rusty-nail birds).

Miles and Directions

0.0 Start at parking lot kiosk. Follow the common trail marked with green and yellow blazes.

0.4 The North Loop splits off to the left. Go straight.

1.0 The South Loop Trail turns right, following the yellow blazes.

2.5 Cross boardwalk over marshy area.

3.8 Reach a fenceline and a kiosk with information about sandhill cranes.

4.2 Arrive back at the parking lot.

More Information

Local Information
Orlando/Orange County Convention and Visitors Bureau: www.orlandoinfo.com.
Kissimmee/Osceola County Chamber of Commerce: www.kissimmeechamber .com.

Local Events/Attractions
Fort Christmas Historical Park contains exhibits on the Seminole Indian Wars: www.nbbd.com/godo/FortChristmas.

Lodging
Orlando/Orange County Convention and Visitors Bureau: www.orlandoinfo.com.
Kissimmee Convention & Visitors Bureau: www.floridakiss.com/rec/hiking/index.php.

Camping
Camping is available at adjacent Moss Park, operated by Orange County.

Florida Wildlife & Conservation Commission: http://myfwc.com/recreation/split_oak.
Osceola County Department of Parks & Recreation: www.osceola.org/index
.cfm?IsFuses=department/Parks.
Orange County Parks & Recreation Department: www.orangecountyfl.net/dept/cesrvcs/parks/
Default.asp.

*Old tree stumps like this one are often the aftermath of a lightning strike, which fells the tree
within a year or two.*

The Florida National Scenic Trail will eventually comprise about 1,800 miles of trail.

Located in Seminole County between the towns of Oviedo and Seminole, the 180-acre Geneva Wilderness Area offers a good variety of scenery as its system of red-blazed loop trails cross and border a shallow pond and travel into pastures and swampland. The native plant communities range from mixed hardwood swamp and mesic hammocks (sort of in-between a dry and wet hammock) to xeric oak, or low-growing oaks punctuated with bare white sand areas. Animals you could sight here include gopher tortoise, white-tailed deer, wild turkey, and grey fox.

For a much longer walk than these loops, you could use this trail system to begin an extended hike all the way to the Little-Big Econ River. Both the Geneva Wilderness Area and Little-Big Econ State Forest have access to the blue-blazed Flagler Trail, which runs north-south through this region and across the Little-Big Econ River. It takes about three hours to make the Little-Big Econ circuit using the

Geneva Wilderness Area trailhead. It's not a trek many make since there are shorter routes to the river; all the more reason to attempt it if you're looking for a relatively remote walk in this crowded region.

Nearest town: Geneva
Start: Just off State Road 426 south of the town of Geneva
Distance: 1.8 miles round-trip with option to add another mile
Approximate hiking time: 2 to 3 hours, depending on routes
Difficulty: Easy to moderate, depending on wetness
Trail surface: Natural surface, bridges
Seasons: Fall through spring
Other trail users: Bikers and horse riders possible

Canine compatibility: Dogs must be leashed
Land status: County natural land
Fees and permits: None
Schedule: Open daylight hours. The Ed Yarborough Nature Center is open the first Saturday of the month from 9:00 a.m. to noon; (407) 665-7432.
Maps: Available online at www.seminolecountyfl.gov/leisure/natland/geneva.asp
Trail contacts: Seminole County Natural Lands Planning & Development; (407) 665-7432 or www.seminolecountyfl.gov/leisure/natland/geneva.asp

Finding the trailhead: Located on SR 426 (Oviedo Road) just south of the town of Geneva. From Interstate 4, exit in Longwood at Highway 434 and go east for 13 miles to Oviedo. Turn left onto SR 426 and go west for about 6 miles, passing the Little-Econ State Forest. The Geneva Wilderness Area is located at 3501 North State Road 426, on the right. The turnoff to parking at the site is Eagle Trail. **GPS:** N28 42.528' W081 07.438'

The Hike

Two main trails are marked with red blazes. The short loop trail is blazed in red and takes thirty to forty-five minutes to complete. A shallow pond in the middle of the property can be a great spot for wildlife during dry periods—if the ponds themselves don't dry up. They've come close during periods of drought but then refill when the rains return and the water table rises. If you examine the shoreline closely you may see small plants that look like strawberry or orange jam. They're actually sundews, tiny carnivorous plants working their best to hold down the local insect population.

▶ Although none of its residents claim Swiss heritage, the ancestry of Geneva residents is amazingly diverse: German, 23.8 percent; English, 17.1 percent; Irish, 13.5 percent; American, 9.0 percent; Scottish, 7.3 percent; Italian, 4.1 percent.

Using the route outlined below, it's less than a mile to the South Camp, the best of the two available group camping areas. This spot is shaded by large oaks, and restrooms and drinkable water are a short distance away on your right. If it's not too dry, you may even find wood available for a campfire.

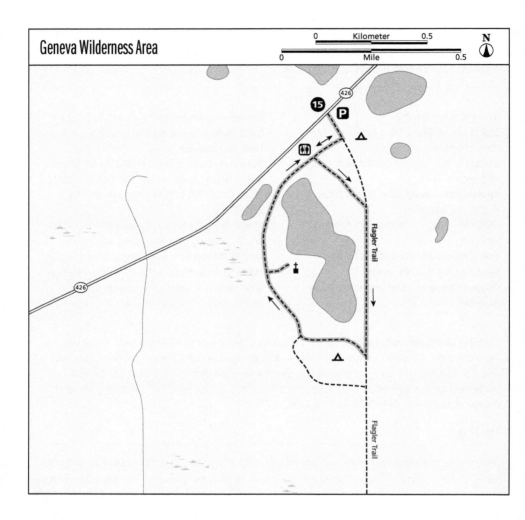

At the southern camping area, you can extend your hike by taking the yellow-blazed path to join the blue-blazed Flagler Trail, then walk south about 1.4 miles to reach the Little-Big Econ State Forest and cross the river bridge there. Allow three to four hours total for this walk, from Geneva Wilderness Area parking lot, start to finish.

The Flagler Trail is a historic route following an old abandoned railroad bed built in 1914 by magnate Henry Flagler for the Florida East Coast Railroad. After the failure of his plan to sell acreage near Chuluota to northern settlers, he stopped rail operations in the area. The state purchased the land to build State Road 13, which never materialized. Seminole County acquired the abandoned rail corridor in 1984. The Florida Trail Organization has designated the southern end part of the Florida National Scenic Trail (FNST). It is possible to follow the Flagler Trail south to the town of Chuluota on a fairly straight pathway.

If you stay on the loop trail at the Southern Camp, you'll turn right to keep paralleling the pond. You'll soon encounter a 0.2-mile side trail going off to the right to the scout group camping area where you'll find a chapel used for interdenominational services. Returning to the main trail, go right to encounter a set of restrooms that mark both the end and start of the loop trail. Continue straight past the trail junction to return to the parking lot for a total of 1.8 miles.

Miles and Directions

0.0 Start from information kiosk. Approach junction of Flagler Trail (yellow diamond blazes) with the featured loop trail (blue diamond blazes). Go right to start the loop trail.

0.3 Arrive at restrooms. Loop trail officially starts here. At the trailhead, go left, then bear right to follow the loop trail as it parallels the pond shoreline.

0.7 Arrive at southern primitive camping area. Go right (west) to return to parking lot. To join Flagler Trail, continue south.

1.0 Side trail on right (0.2 mile each way) leads to chapel at the pond.

1.4 Staying on the loop trail, arrive back at restroom area. This marks end of loop trail. Go straight (left) to return to parking lot.

1.8 End at the parking lot.

More Information

Local Information and Lodging

Seminole County government: www.seminolecountyfl.gov/guide/visitor.asp
Seminole County Convention and Visitors Bureau: www.visitseminole.com/tourism-cvb/guide.asp.
City of Oviedo: www.ci.oviedo.fl.us.
Greater Oviedo Chamber of Commerce: www.oviedochamber.org/.

Local Attractions

Several other wilderness areas are located within easy driving distance:

The 475-acre **Lake Proctor Wilderness Area** has 6 miles of trails featuring sand pine scrub, pine flatwoods, sandhill, and bayhead swamp: www.seminolecountyfl.gov/leisure/natland/proctor.asp.

The 240-acre **Econ River Wilderness Area,** just south of the city of Oviedo and on the western bank of the Econ River, has 3 miles of trails meandering through pine flatwoods, sandhill, and river swamp. Wildlife here includes the great horned owl, white-tailed deer, and golden mouse; www .seminolecountyfl.gov/leisure/natland/econ.asp.

The 490-acre **Lake Jesup Wilderness Area** has a 3-mile multiuse trail leading to the lake's extensive flood plain with a good view of the birdlife that lives there; www.seminolecountyfl.gov/ leisure/natland/jesup.asp.

Camping

Primitive camping by the river is allowed at Little-Big Econ State Forest with a permit.

Organizations

Seminole County Natural Lands Planning and Development: www.seminolecountyfl.gov/pd (Planning and Development home page) or www.seminolecountyfl.gov/leisure/natland (Natural Lands home page).

Plume hunters answering the latest fashion for women's hats severely depleted the snowy egret population, which has since bounced back.

16 Little-Big Econ State Forest: Kolokee Loop Trail

The easy hike through the Little-Big Econ State Forest often attracts groups of hikers.

The 5,048-acre forest is part of a wildlife-roaming corridor, including the Tosohatchee Wildlife Management Area and other state lands that will create a 100-mile-long wildlife passage from State Road 46 and the Florida Turnpike. The Econlockhatchee River, a name that normally is shortened simply to the "Econ," is a blackwater river that meanders through some of the least developed parts of central Florida, a region where open spaces are becoming more and more of a premium. About half the hike parallels the Econ River, which can be fished from the bank. The Econ is a designated Outstanding Florida Waterway, deemed worthy of special protection because of its natural attributes. This hike is one of the region's best waterway walks, with several primitive campsites. You have two choices: the state forest's Kolokee Trail described here or a longer hike on a segment of the Florida National Scenic Trail (FNST). The trails overlap only slightly.

Nearest town: Oviedo
Start: Kiosk at the Barr Street parking lot
Distance: 4.8-mile loop
Approximate hiking time: 3 to 4 hours
Difficulty: Easy unless the trail is muddy
Trail surface: Primarily dirt path
Seasons: October through May generally the most comfortable
Other trail users: Cyclists and equestrians on designated trails, which hikers sometimes use; hiking trail limited to foot traffic
Canine compatibility: Leashed dogs permitted

Land status: State forest
Fees and permits: Day-use fee under $5; primitive camping permit required
Schedule: Open sunrise to sunset; hunting permitted on the Kilbee Tract only, which does not adjoin this section
Maps: Sometimes available at the parking lot information kiosk, but none required
Trail contact: Division of Forestry, Little-Big Econ State Forest, 1350 Snow Hill Road, Geneva FL 32732; (407) 971-3500; www .fl-dof.com/state_forests/little_big_econ.html

Finding the trailhead: The forest is located between the small towns of Chuluota and Geneva in eastern Seminole County. Coming from the west (Geneva or Oviedo), take CR 426 (Oviedo Road) to Barr Street, 3.3 miles east of Oviedo. The state forest signs make the parking lot easily identifiable. **GPS:** N28 41.245' W081 09.558'

The Hike

The "little" and "big" Econ designations refer to the varying sizes of the river, which in some places is akin to a narrow winding stream and in others a true, classic river. Wildlife viewing here consists primarily of birds, but the species are classic: bald eagles, ospreys, roseate spoonbills, and sandhill cranes. Deer and turkeys are also good possibilities.

Trail maps sometimes are available at the parking lot information kiosk. You'll encounter different trail systems with different blazes: orange for hiking, white for multiuse, and blue for a cross section of the Flagler Trail that continues north into the Geneva Wilderness Area. It's not uncommon to meet cyclists where the trails intersect and especially on an optional return loop trail, where they overlap.

To follow the Kolokee Trail, part of the State Forest Trailwalker Program, take the well-marked white-blazed trail until it intersects the orange-blazed FNST. The white-blazed route is your optional return if you choose to make a longer loop hike by joining a multiuse trail.

You'll pass through an open field before entering the woods. The river is off to your right. You can approach the river more closely than the trail in some areas, but the trail keeps to the high ground to avoid wet areas when the Econ is rain swollen.

This path goes through some of central Florida's most remarkable, unspoiled scenery and hugs the riverbank in many places. There are lots of places to fish from the bank. This is a wonderful spot for a weekend escape, and a campsite waits near the river.

▶ When you visit Little-Big Econ State Forest, stop at the nearby Black Hammock Restaurant (www.theblackhammock.com) for some pretty good fish camp food.

Little-Big Econ State Forest

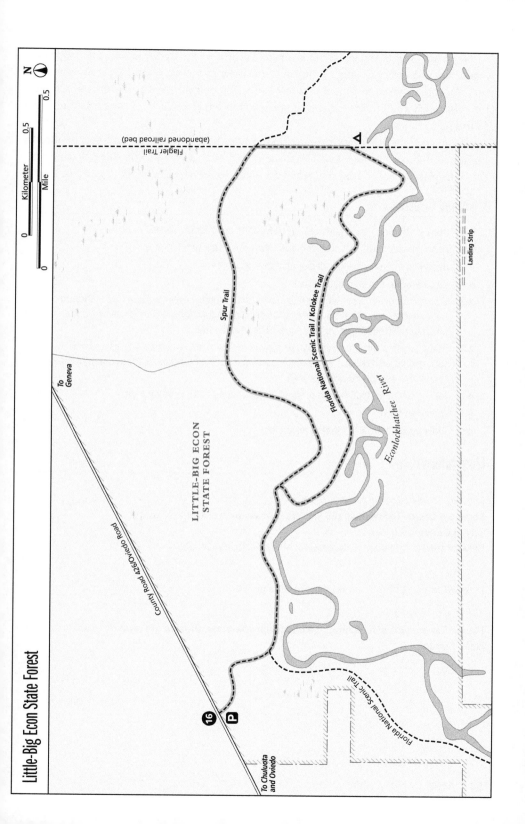

Little-Big Econ State Forest

LITTLE-BIG ECON
STATE FOREST

Econlockhatchee River

Florida National Scenic Trail / Kolokee Trail

Spur Trail

Flagler Trail (abandoned railroad bed)

County Road A26/Oviedo Road

To Geneva

To Chuluota and Oviedo

Florida National Scenic Trail

Landing Strip

16

P

N

Kilometer
0   0.5
0   0.5
Mile

To avoid cyclists and equestrians entirely, return to the trailhead the same way you came. If you'd prefer a longer loop hike and want to see more of the forest, turn left (north) at the junction with the blue-blazed Flagler Trail. When you encounter the junction with a white-blazed multiuse trail, turn left (west) for an immediate return to the parking lot.

If you go right (east) you'll end up on the 1.4-mile bike trail that leads to a trailhead on Snowhill Road. Some hikers like this option and arrange a pickup there. Staying on the blue-blazed Flagler Trail will take you north to the Geneva Wilderness Area.

Miles and Directions

0.0   Start at the Barr Street parking lot. Follow white state forest blazes.

0.1   Reach junction with the orange-blazed FNST; turn right to follow the FNST.

0.3   Reach an open field and a designated camping area.

0.7   Cross a white-blazed multiuse trail.

2.3   Reach a camping area with fire ring just north of a bridge over the Econ River. (**Option:** Retrace your steps to avoid returning via a multiuse trail, for a 4.6-mile out-and-back hike.) Turn left (north) to join the blue-blazed Flagler Trail.

2.6   At the junction with the white-blazed bicycle trail, turn left onto the white-blazed trail. (Going right will take you to the state forest main office on Snowhill Road. Some hikers like to add this section for a longer walk.)

4.5   Taking the return loop blazed in white, pass an open-field camping area.

4.7   Cross the FNST.

4.8   Arrive back at the Barr Street parking lot.

More Information

Local Information and Lodging

Seminole County Convention and Visitors Bureau: www.visitseminole.com.
City of Oviedo: www.ci.oviedo.fl.us.
Greater Oviedo Chamber of Commerce: www.oviedochamber.org.

Camping

Primitive camping by the river is allowed with a permit.

Organizations

Florida Department of Agriculture and Consumer Services, Division of Forestry: www.fl-dof.com/state_forests/.

17 Disney Wilderness Preserve Trails

A fanny pack is all you need for carrying snacks and drinks on Central Florida's shorter trails.

Despite its name, this 12,000–acre tract is not part of the huge Disney World holding. Instead, it is owned and managed by The Nature Conservancy (TNC), which is returning the property to more of a wetlands condition. Disney's name is connected to the preserve thanks to the U.S. Clean Water Act, which requires wetlands damaged by human activity to be mitigated (replaced) elsewhere. The Disney Preserve is a mitigation project established in 1992 with an initial purchase of 8,500 acres. More acreage has since been added by other businesses that also had to compensate for disturbing natural wetlands areas. Their names, however, have not been added to the preserve's title, perhaps to their relief. Six miles of hiking and interpretive trails are laid out on about 700 acres.

Nearest town: Poinciana
Start: TNC Conservation Learning Center
Distance: Two loop trails creating a hike of 5.4 miles
Approximate hiking time: 2 to 3 hours
Difficulty: Easy
Trail surface: Surfaced and dirt paths

Seasons: Dry, cooler months, generally November to May
Other trail users: Hikers only; smoking prohibited on the trails
Canine compatibility: Pets prohibited
Land status: Privately owned by The Nature Conservancy

Fees and permits: $3 per person for the general public, $2 for TNC members who present their membership card
Schedule: Open 9:00 a.m. to 5:00 p.m. daily October through May; weekdays only the rest of the year

Maps: Available on-site
Trail contact: The Disney Wilderness Preserve, 6075 Scrub Jay Trail, Kissimmee, FL 34759; (407) 935-0002; www.nature.org/florida. Prairie Lakes Trails are sometimes closed due to flooding or restoration activities. Call ahead.

Finding the trailhead: From Interstate 4, take the State Road 535 exit and go south to Poinciana Boulevard. Turn right (south) and go to the end of the road, about 15 miles, and then turn right onto Pleasant Hill Road. Proceed approximately 0.25 mile, turn left onto Old Pleasant Hill Road. Go 0.5 mile to Scrub Jay Trail. Turn left and follow Scrub Jay Trail to The Nature Conservancy's Conservation Learning Center. **GPS:** N28 07.726' W081 25.810'

The Hike

Because this is a wetlands area, expect to find the trails muddy and sloppy during the rainy season. Many parts are also quite open, so wear a hat and take water (and bug repellent). Leaving the visitor center, you'll pass one of the wetlands projects, a two-acre lake that should attract bird life up close, within a few yards of the trail. You'll encounter a second information "chickee" where a side trail splits off to the left.

This is a 0.5-mile interpretive trail loop through a pine flatwoods. An excellent booklet describes nineteen marked features, such as a gopher tortoise burrow used by more than 600 different animal species—including mice, snakes, lizards, and insects—as both an emergency shelter from fire and shelter from the hot Florida sun.

Returning to the main access, go left to access the two main hiking trails. You'll start on the 2.5-mile Blue Loop Trail, which eventually joins the longer Red Loop Trail to cover a combined distance of 5.4 miles. At the Blue Trail trailhead junction, bear to the left, which shortly will bring you to a side trail to Lake Russell, also on your left. This is where you want to be first thing in the morning for a chance to see otters and ospreys. The gnarled cypress trees are especially photogenic. Relax and enjoy the view from one of the picnic tables.

▶ Disney Wilderness Preserve supports a wide variety of plant life, but the bird life, many of them permanent residents, is even better. The best bird-watching is in winter, when the migratory species visit—not to be confused with the simultaneous migration of human "snow birds."

Return to the main Blue Trail and turn left. Before long you will junction with the Red Trail, which circles a bay swamp. You also have the option to stay on the Blue Trail and take a shortcut trail on your right leading to a bench at the end of the Red Trail, completely bypassing that section. But why leave anything out?

Taking the Red Trail, you'll walk through a series of oak hammocks, eventually reaching a bench under one of the shaded trees—a nice spot to relax and take a sip of water. Continuing, the trail moves from oak hammocks to border a huge

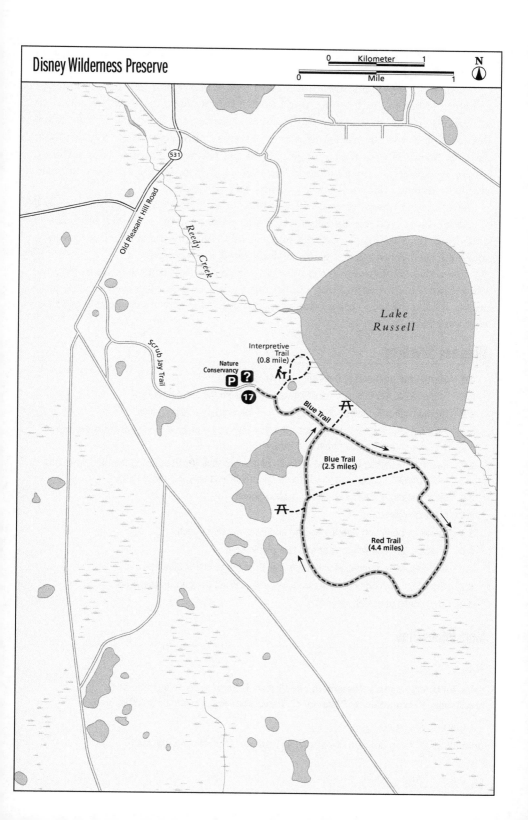

marshland with a variety of bay trees off to your right. This section is one reason why you brought repellent.

Farther on is a picnic table on a short side trail veering left. To continue, go straight, and before much longer you'll reach a bench where the Red Trail junctions with the Blue. Go left to return to the visitor center on the Blue Trail via one of the dirt roads that cross the hiking paths at several spots. This is one of the few dirt roads open to hikers. If you don't spot deer from the hiking paths, don't give up hope. You're just as likely to see them bounding over the field as you drive to the entry gate. Bambi's children, your own kids may claim. And why not?

Most of the Disney Preserve's 12,000-plus acres are being used for restoration and research projects, and it is unlikely that the trail system will be expanded. That's hardly a hardship, since hiking the present system easily consumes most of a day. One nice touch are the cypress-shaded picnic tables located at two points.

The only potable water in the preserve is at the visitor center; be sure to have full water bottles before setting out. Unlike most other Disney-related territories, there are no drink stands, ice-cream vendors, or hot dog sellers anywhere about—and that's very, very nice.

Miles and Directions

0.0   Start at the trailhead at the visitor center.

0.1   At the kiosk, the 0.5-mile Pine Flatwoods Trail is on the left. Go straight.

0.3   The trail splits. Go left on the Blue Trail and follow the LAKE RUSSELL sign.

0.4   Pass the spur trail to Lake Russell. (**FYI:** The lake is the place to be first thing in the morning for a chance to see otters and ospreys.)

1.7   Reach the junction of the Red Trail with blue cross trail. (**Option:** Taking the blue cross trail back creates a loop walk of 3.2 miles. The full hike is only 2.2 miles longer.)

2.0   Pass a stand of oak trees, and a shaded bench.

2.6   Make a sharp turn.

3.4   Come to a junction with a jeep trail and pass another bench.

4.0   Reach a junction with a spur trail to a picnic area.

4.2   Red Trail ends at junction with Blue Trail. Bear left to follow Blue Trail out.

5.1   The loop walk ends near the LAKE RUSSELL sign. Go left to return to the visitor center.

5.4   Arrive back at the visitor center.

More Information

Local Information

Orlando/Orange County Convention and Visitors Bureau: www.orlandoinfo.com.
Kissimmee/Osceola County Chamber of Commerce: www.kissimmeechamber.com.

Local Events/Attractions

Off-road buggy tours are held on Sunday at 1:30 p.m., October through May.

Lodging

Orlando/Orange County Convention and Visitors Bureau: www.orlandoinfo.com.
Kissimmee/Osceola County Chamber of Commerce: www.kissimmeechamber.com.

Camping

The closest camping facilities are commercial campgrounds close to the theme parks.

Organizations

The Nature Conservancy: www.nature.org. This preserve is a good place to learn more about TNC. More than any other conservation organization, TNC puts its money where its mouth is by purchasing land both above and below water all over the world. At this writing, that totals 11 million acres in North America alone—a figure that will be considerably larger by the time you read this guide. Regardless of where you live, TNC is a good organization to belong to and support. They actually accomplish what others only talk about.

18 Hillsborough River State Park: River Rapids, Baynard, and Florida Trails

Not very impressive but this is the largest set of rapids in Central Florida.

Hillsborough River is famous for its two small sets of rapids created by outcrops of Suwannee limestone. Although not a cause for excitement for most visitors, the chance to hear rapids while hiking (or boating) is virtually unknown in Florida. These are ranked as Florida's only Class II rapids, but that rating seems generous. The river does flow fairly swiftly here, and swimming is not permitted. The 3,738-acre park features a Florida National Scenic Trail (FNST) loop of just over 3 miles as well as short nature trails, combining for a possible total of 7.3 miles through one of Florida's most scenic state parks. The featured hike below of 5.8 miles links the River Rapids, Baynard, and Florida Trails.

Nearest town: Thonotosassa
Start: Northeast corner of the parking lot
Distance: 5.8-mile lollipop
Approximate hiking time: 3 hours
Difficulty: Easy

Trail surface: Natural surface, boardwalk; often wet after summer rains
Seasons: Fall through spring; often crowded in summer
Other trail users: Nature lovers

Canine compatibility: Leashed pets permitted
Land status: State park
Fees and permits: Park admission fee under $5
Schedule: Open 8:00 a.m. until sunset

Maps: Available at the park office
Trail contact: Hillsborough River State Park, 15402 U.S. 301, Thonotosassa, FL 33592; (813) 987-6771; www.floridastateparks.org/ hillsboroughriver

Finding the trailhead: Hillsborough River State Park is located 9 miles north of Tampa and 6 miles south of Zephyrhills on U.S. Highway 301. Park at the parking lot on the right, located several hundred yards after the turnoff to the Fort Foster Museum.

Coming southbound from Ocala on Interstate 75: Take exit 279 (State Road 54) east to US 301. Travel south on US 301 for 6 miles; the park will be on your right.

Going I-75 northbound from Tampa: Take exit 265 (Fowler Avenue) east to US 301. Travel north for 9 miles; the park will be on your left.

Traveling westbound on Interstate 4: Take exit 10 to County Road 579. Follow CR 579 north to US 301. Following the signs, go north 7 miles; the park will be on your left.

Traveling I-4 eastbound: Take exit 7 (be careful of the merges) and go north on US 301 for 14 miles; the park will be on your left. **GPS:** N28 08.916' W082 14.055'

The Hike

The walk to the rapids is not part of the FNST segment but belongs to the River Rapids Nature Trail. From the trailhead follow the short path that leads to the first set of rapids, only 0.2 mile from the trailhead. Go straight to the rapids, then bear left. You will use boardwalks in some areas and pass the remnants of others on what is the park's original trail.

The path borders the river until you reach the suspension bridge. Cross the river to start the Baynard Trail, named for the park's first superintendent. The trail quickly turns inland, away from the river. It's now only about a mile on the Baynard Trail to the FNST loop, which offers primitive camping.

You reach the junction with the FNST after 1.5 miles where a Florida Trail sign points off to the right. (If necessary, you can end your hike at this point by going straight ahead and crossing a bridge leading to a picnic area.) Go right to follow the blue blazes on a short access path to the Florida Trail. When you junction with it, turn right to walk counterclockwise, following the familiar orange blazes for the next 3.3 miles.

▶ Hillsborough is named for nobleman Wills Hills (1718–1793). Hills, the Earl of Hillsborough, was instrumental in giving Great Britain control of Florida in general and the Tampa Bay area in particular.

In just a mile (2.5 miles total since the hike began) you'll reach the side trail leading to a primitive campsite located in one of the trail's high and dryer spots. Continuing the trail will yo-yo up and down, from dry stretches of white sand down to black mud and, in some places, taking a bridge to cross what otherwise would be too messy to contemplate seriously.

Hillsborough River State Park

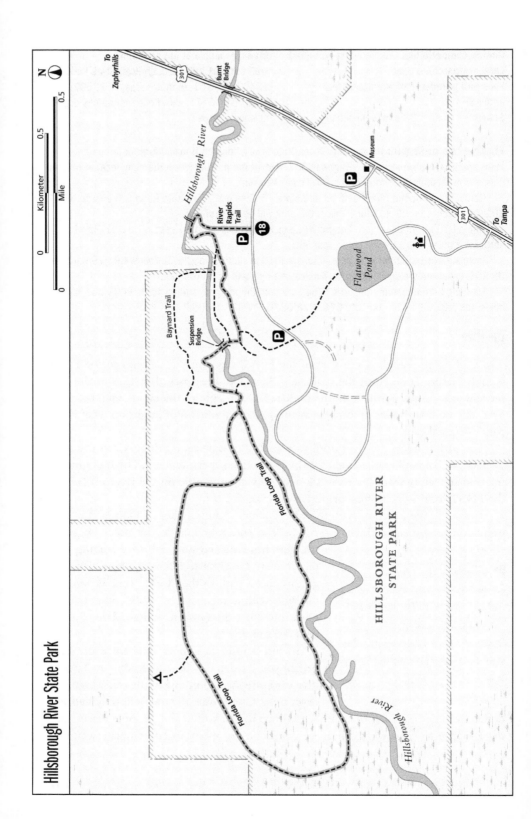

Slowly the trail starts back toward the Hillsborough River, reaching a small bluff above the stream at 3.4 miles.

From this point the path follows beside the river for a short distance, sometimes passing over some of its feeder creeks, before turning away and taking several bridges as the trail climbs steadily higher, ending at 4.8 miles. Take the 0.1-mile blue-blazed access trail to rejoin the Baynard Trail on your return via a different route that doesn't cross the river.

The trail can be quite wet—the reason for a series of bridges on the rest of the FNST until it ends—reconnecting with the Baynard Trail loop at a different point and with different scenery than on the first leg. This section starts away from the river but then parallels it and returns to the suspension bridge. From there you can take a shorter route back to the parking lot or retrace your initial River Rapids route, which most people do. As small as they are, the rapids are still something special in the normally flat Florida landscape.

The river plain and pine flatwoods house such wildlife as otters, deer, wild turkeys, pileated woodpeckers, red-shouldered hawks, and barred owls. A walk under the dense old-growth tree canopy here beside the lively Hillsborough River is one of the most memorable jaunts in Florida.

Miles and Directions

0.0 Start at parking lot trailhead and follow the blue-blazed trail.

0.2 Reach a shelter and the first set of rapids. Go left.

0.3 Cross boardwalk over a cypress swamp.

0.6 Cross the river on a suspension bridge and turn left to start the Baynard Trail.

0.8 The trail turns inland.

1.5 Begin the Florida Trail loop, marked by orange blazes. Turn right to follow the trail counterclockwise.

1.9 Reach a bridge crossing over a wet area.

2.5 Come to another bridge crossing and the junction with 0.1-mile blue-blazed trail to a primitive campsite. Stay on the orange-blazed trail.

3.0 Cross another wet area on a bridge.

3.4 Emerge on a bluff overlooking the Hillsborough River.

4.0 Cross another bridge.

4.8 End the Florida Trail loop and rejoin new section of Baynard Trail.

5.2 Return to the suspension bridge.

5.6 Return to the rapids.

5.8 Arrive back at the parking lot.

More Information

Local Information
Tampa Bay Convention and Visitors Bureau: www.visittampabay.com.

Local Events/Attractions
The Fort Foster Historic Site, a reconstructed 1837 fort manned during the Second Seminole War, is located within the park. It is the only standing replica of a Second Seminole War Fort in the nation. Guided tours are offered on Saturday at 2:00 p.m. and on Sunday at 11:00 a.m. by advance reservation: www.floridastateparks.org/fortfoster/.

Other park amenities include a half-acre man-made swimming area, bicycle trails, kayaking, canoeing, and fishing (license required).

Lodging
The closest accommodations to the park are in Zephyrhills and Thonotosassa: www.visittampa bay .com.

Camping
The park has 108 campsites for tents and RVs. Reservations: (800) 326-3521; www.reserve america.com/index.jsp.

Organizations
Florida Department of Environmental Protection, Division of Recreation and Parks: www.dep .state.fl.us/parks.

19 Tiger Creek Preserve: The Pfundstein Trail

The swamp lily is one of the signature plants on the Pfundstein Trail near Patrick Creek.

The Nature Conservancy (TNC) protects this 4,869-acre gem that borders the edge of Florida's oldest and highest landmass, the venerable Lake Wales Ridge. Considered the most ancient part of the state, the Lake Wales Ridge is an enormous sand hill running north and south. Some experts believe it was the first place to emerge after the ocean covering the Florida peninsula receded. Others contend that this narrow ridge was not covered by waves but was an isolated island where plants and animals evolved in isolation.

Either scenario would explain why the Ridge contains one of the largest collections of rare organisms in the world with perhaps the highest concentration of rare and endangered plants in the continental United States. Animals residing here include sand skinks, gopher tortoises, the Florida mouse, indigo snakes, and gopher frogs. Among the rare plants found here are the scrub plum, pygmy fringe tree, and Carter's mustard.

Established in 1971, the preserve is named for Tiger Creek, an unspoiled blackwater stream that cuts through the heart of the sanctuary. The land surrounding it includes hardwood swamps, hammocks, oak scrub, pine flatwoods, sandhill, and longleaf pine/wiregrass habitat. Two hikes are available, the quick and easy thirty-minute George Cooley Trail and the much longer Pfundstein Trail, described here.

Nearest town: Babson Park
Start: Small parking lot at the trailhead gate
Distance: 8.3 miles
Approximate hiking time: 4 hours
Difficulty: Easy
Trail surface: Natural
Seasons: Fall through spring
Other trail users: Nature lovers
Canine compatibility: No pets
Land status: Private preserve open to the public
Fees and permits: None required

Schedule: Open during daylight hours
Maps: Available from the Florida Trail Association and at the trailhead kiosk
Trail contact: The Tiger Creek Center, operated by TNC, is intended to help Floridians not only understand the important natural role fire plays in the state's ecology but how to live amidst Florida's flammable landscape. The Center is open Monday through Friday, 9:00 a.m. to 5:00 p.m., except federal holidays. Call (863) 635-7506 for more information; www.nature.org/florida.

Finding the trailhead: From the town of Babson Park, take State Road 17 south for 2 miles. Turn left onto Murray Road. Go 2 miles and turn left onto Pfundstein Road. The main parking area is about 100 yards ahead. Walk through the gate to access the trail. The Cooley Trail, a short hike not described here, is on the left shortly after you turn onto Pfundstein Road. **GPS:** N27 48.479' W081 29.523'

The Hike

The small parking lot is located outside a metal gate that is likely to be locked. No problem; simply walk around and through the cattle guard. Now begin your walk that will take you on a side trail across Patrick Creek and then into the region known as the Central Highlands.

To appreciate this unique region you're walking through, it helps to have a better understanding of how it was formed and why its preservation is so important. Tiger Creek Preserve is one small section of the Lake Wales Ridge in Polk and Highlands Counties. The ecosystems here are small remnants of ancient flora and fauna that used to be far more widespread, an exceptional and irreplaceable habitat in global terms. The most famous and arguably most important is Florida's ancient interior scrubland characterized by deep sands punctuated with upland, marsh, and sinkhole lakes sprinkled between sections of pine flatwoods. An estimated forty plant and vertebrate species live here, including seventeen species listed for federal protection and more than a dozen more proposed for federal listing as endangered or threatened.

Like the better known Galapagos Islands, the ridge is composed of ancient beach and sand

▶ The Nature Conservancy (TNC) is one of the most effective protectors of the environment, preserving plants, animals, and natural communities through positive action. It purchases sensitive land areas and stewards them until a state or federal agency is able to buy the land then uses proceeds from the sale to purchase more land. TNC protects land in all fifty states and thirty countries worldwide. In Florida, its holdings include 1.1 million acres. Visit the Web site at www.nature.org.

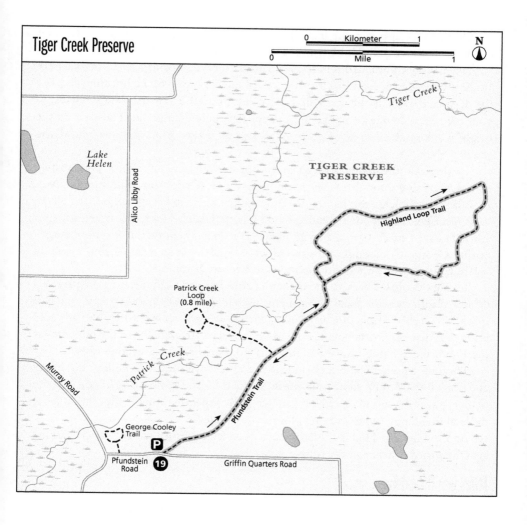

dunes formed perhaps 1 and 3 million years ago. This region was sporadically isolated from North America by rising sea levels during ice ages, cutting off plants and
animals from the North American continent for such long periods that some species
developed differences. Their variations continued after the Ridge was rejoined with
North America.

The land here is tough and harsh, illustrated by how the sand skink lives. Living
between rosemary scrub and palmetto-pine flatwoods, the skink relies on moisture
existing underneath tree bark and in sand starting about 1 inch below the surface.
Consequently, for its nourishment the sand skink remains in underground burrows
just under the sand where everything it needs to survive is most easily accessible. With
a transparent lid over its eyes, the sand skink is classified as the only sand-swimming
lizard in North America.

On this hike, it pays to be like Sherlock Holmes and pay attention to the tiniest details such as the sand skink's winding tracks through the sand.

Like a modern beach, this is dry, open, sandy terrain, Florida's version of a desert. Ironically, this desert receives Florida's normal rainfall (up to 50 inches annually), but the deep sand soaks up the water almost instantly. You need to carry plenty of water of your own, wear a wide-brimmed hat and, most definitely, sunglasses. The glare off the bright white sand, made up of grains of ancient quartzite, could give you a headache without them.

Starting out, this orange-blazed section of the Florida Trail almost immediately turns left, passing through an area attempting to restore cutthroat grass found only in Florida. Fairly quickly this lightly used track junctions with a jeep trail bearing left to cross Patrick Creek. If you're willing to get muddy, take this short side trail leading to a bridge over Patrick Creek, a more interesting stream here than it is on the neighboring George Cooley hike. On the other side of the bridge, you'll find a muddy 0.3-mile loop walk through marshland and then dry hammock.

Taking the bridge back to the main trail, turn left and walk toward a singular section of plant earth, the Lake Wales highlands. Going left at the trail junction, you'll pass small scrubby plants that may have yellow flowers: St. John's wort, popularly sold for its anti depressant attributes. Some of these species are endemic to the preserve, far more valuable as living plants than the crushed ingredients of a vitamin capsule.

The trail through these highlands is not always well marked. Follow the blazes and don't be misled by game trails made by the local deer population. If you lose the orange blazes for too long, retrace your steps. Be especially careful after 3.8 miles as the trail frequently twists and turns for the next mile.

At 5.6 miles, the Highlands Loop ends. Turn left to return directly to the parking area for a total distance of 7.6 miles.

Miles and Directions

0.0 Depart from parking lot. Follow the orange blazes leaving from the left side of Pfundstein Road.

0.7 Blue-blazed 200-yard side trail to the left leads to bridge crossing Patrick Creek and 0.3-mile Great Sand Pine Loop. For main trail, continue straight.

1.1 Assuming you've taken the Patrick Creek side trail, go left when you return to the main trail. If you didn't take this detour, deduct 0.4 mile from the distances detailed below.

2.6 Main trail, sometimes called West Hickory Trail, arrives at junction with return trail coming in from the right. Continue straight and then bear right (east) on the northernmost section of the Highlands Loop.

3.2 Bear left (north) as loop trail begins following service road.

3.7 Trail makes the first series of turns to the right. Follow blazes carefully.

4.3 Follow service road, then turn right.

4.7 Trail begins a series of zigzags. Pay close attention to blazes.

5.3 Follow trail to the right to service road.

5.6 Turn left onto access trail and begin retracing steps back to parking area.

6.9 Junction with Great Sand Loop Trail on the left. Continue straight.

7.6 Terminus at parking lot.

More Information

Local Information

The nonprofit Polk Partners contains a collection of Web links about Polk County: www.nytrnghotel .com/ll/polkpartners.

Polk County Convention and Visitors Bureau: www.sunsational.org.

Local Events/Attractions

The Lake Wales Ridge State Forest near the town of Frostproof contains several hiking trails, including 20 miles of the Florida Trail; (863) 635-8589; www.fl-dof.com/state_forests/lake_wales_ridge.html.

Lodging

Polk County Convention and Visitors Bureau: www.sunsational.org.

Camping

Primitive camping is available in the nearby Lake Wales Ridge State Forest; (863) 635-8589; www .fl-dof.com/state_forests/lake_wales_ridge.html.

Organizations

The Nature Conservancy: www.nature.org.

Overnight Hikes

20 Blue Spring State Park: Pine Island Trail

Beware any raccoon that seems aggressive or unafraid of people since rabies is always a concern.

The entry in Short Family Hikes for the Boardwalk Trail in Blue Spring State Park near Orlando described the history of the West Indian manatee and the boardwalk trail beside the spring run that the endangered mammals inhabit during the cool winter months. Now it's time to get into the real outdoors and a true wilderness hike through an undisturbed area bordering the St. Johns River. You'll end up at a primitive campsite beside the river.

Nearest town: Orange City
Start: Parking lot bordering the St. Johns River
Distance: 8.0 miles out and back
Approximate hiking time: 4 to 5 hours
Difficulty: Easy to moderate, depending on recent rainfall
Trail surface: Natural surface
Seasons: Fall through spring
Other trail users: Boardwalk wheelchair accessible; hikers only on the forest trail

Canine compatibility: Leashed pets permitted
Land status: State park
Fees and permits: Entrance fee under $5
Schedule: 8:00 a.m. to sunset
Maps: Available at the park
Trail contact: Blue Spring State Park, 2100 West French Avenue, Orange City, FL 32763; (386) 775-3663; www.floridastateparks.org/bluespring

Finding the trailhead: Coming from the east coast, from Interstate 4 between Orlando and Daytona, take exit 114 and follow the Blue Spring State Park signs. Go south on U.S. Highway 17/92 to Orange City, about 2.5 miles. Turn right onto West French Avenue, which leads to the park entrance on the left. Drive to the main parking lot, which overlooks the St. Johns River. The boardwalk borders the river.

Coming from Orlando, on I-4 take exit 111B toward Orange City. Go 0.4 mile and turn right onto Enterprise Road. Drive for 0.9 mile and turn right onto South Volusia Avenue, which turns into North Volusia Avenue in 1.7 miles. Proceed straight on North Volusia for another 0.2 mile, then turn left onto West French Avenue, which leads to the park entrance on the left. Drive to the main parking lot, which overlooks the St. Johns River. The boardwalk borders the river. **GPS:** N28 56.569' W081 20.469'

The Hike

The 4-mile one-way Pine Island Trail hike starts from the main parking lot. The U-shaped trail passes through sand pine scrub, pine flatwoods, and marsh hammock. At the end it follows the edge of a freshwater lagoon that puts you on a bank adjacent to the parking area but about a mile below it. If some sort of bridge spanned the lagoon to provide a crossing, this would become a loop trail. Since there isn't one, you must retrace your steps, for an out-and-back hike of 8 miles.

▶ The largest spring on the St. Johns River, Blue Spring was home for centuries for native Timucuan Indians, who left behind several large shell mounds in the river.

In this instance, separation and isolation become good things. You end up at a spot with four primitive campsites. Because space is limited, you need to sign in upon entering the park if you intend to camp. Since most people will be at the spring run boardwalk, you'll probably have the trail all to yourself unless an organized hiking group happens to show up the same day.

At times this trail can be very wet, with waist-deep water in some places. Check with the park rangers for current conditions—unless you brought a snorkel.

Miles and Directions

0.0 Start at the main (lower) parking lot kiosk.

3.0 The trail descends into the wettest area of the trail.

4.0 Reach the banks of the St. Johns River, your turnaround point. Retrace your steps.

8.0 Arrive back at the main (lower) parking lot kiosk.

More Information

Local Information
Volusia County Tourism: http://echotourism.com.
Orange City: www.ci.orange-city.fl.us.

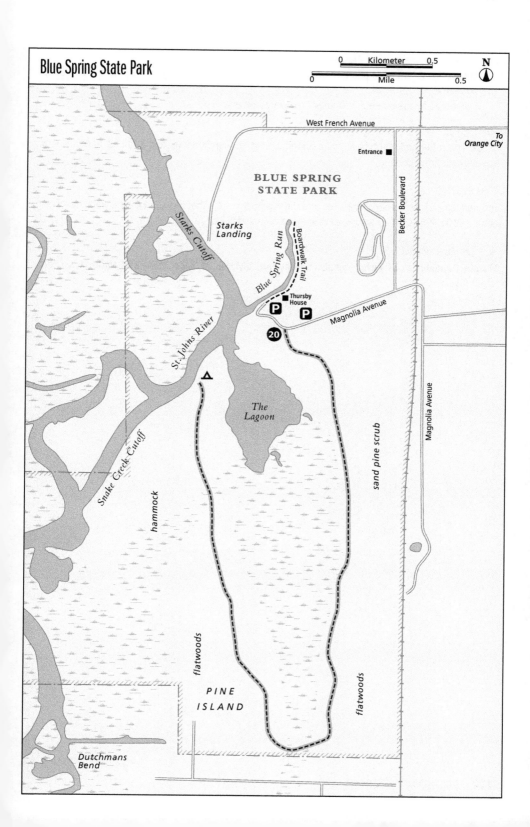

Local Events/Attractions

Rental canoes are available and a narrated scenic boat tour departs once in the morning and early afternoon.

A manatee festival is held in Orange City every January.

Lodging

Six cabins in the park each have two bedrooms, heat, air-conditioning, and a full kitchen. No pets are allowed in the cabins.

Camping

The park has 51 developed campsites and the 4 primitive sites that require a 4-mile walk. Reservations: (800) 326-3521 or www.reserveamerica.com/index.jsp.

Organizations

Florida Department of Environmental Protection, Division of Recreation and Parks: www.dep .state.fl.us.

21 Seminole State Forest: Florida and Lower Wekiva Loop Trails

Orange blazes for the Florida Trail can appear anywhere, including tree stumps.

Located in the all-important Wekiva River Basin, the 25,812-acre Seminole State Forest is one of the last black bear strongholds in central Florida. Around fifty of the animals are believed to move in and out of the basin regularly. The forest contains all thirteen of the region's natural communities, including 1,725 acres of sand pine scrub, a true scarcity outside the Ocala National Forest. The forest contains more than 21 miles of hiking trails, including the featured hike—a section of the Florida National Scenic Trail (FNST) that runs north-south through the length of the forest. There also are three loop trails: River Creek, Sulphur Island, and Paola Loops. The Lower Wekiva Loop Trail and Sulphur Island Loop are included in the Florida Division of Forestry's Trailwalker Program.

Nearest town: Eustis

Start: For both the FNST and the Lower Wekiva Loop, begin from the parking lot at southern end of the forest

Distance: Florida Trail segment, 7.5 miles one-way; for the Lower Wekiva Loop, 9.6 miles includes the walk to join the trail and return to the southern parking lot.

Approximate hiking time: 5 to 6 hours for Florida Trail segment; 10 hours for the Lower Wekiva Loop

Difficulty: Easy to moderate, depending on rainfall

Trail surface: Mostly dirt path

Seasons: Fall through spring; public hunting area

Other trail users: Equestrians, cyclists

Canine compatibility: Leashed dogs permitted

Land status: State forest

Fees and permits: State Forest Use Permits required; must be obtained by phone or in person from the forestry station in Leesburg

Schedule: Day use from sunrise to sunset

Maps: Available on-site

Trail contact: Division of Forestry, Leesburg Forestry Station, 9610 County Road 44, Leesburg, FL 34788; (352) 360-6675; www.fl-dof .com/state_forests/seminole.html

Special considerations: No swimming is permitted in the park.

Finding the trailhead: Access to the north-south running Florida Trail is available at two points. The southern trailhead is off State Road 46 about 14 miles west of Sanford. From Interstate 4, take the 101C exit and go west on SR 46. Access to the forest is on the right after crossing the Wekiva River.

To find the northern trailhead, continue on SR 46 past the southern trailhead, then turn right onto State Road 46A, which ends at County Road 44. Go right onto CR 44 toward the town of Cassia. The northern parking area will be on the right. **GPS:** N28 49.160' W081 25.686'

The Hikes

Florida National Scenic Trail (FNST)

This section of the Florida Trail traverses Sand and Pine Roads and runs for 7.5 miles through the heart of the 1,725-acre Seminole Forest. Appropriately named roads since the sand pine scrub of the area provides ideal habitat for many threatened species such as the Florida black bear, scrub jay, eastern indigo snake, hooded pitcher plant, scrub bay, and scrub holly. Going from south to north, the main trail soon intersects at a Y junction with the white-blazed,

▶ Blackwater Creek takes its name from the water's tannin color, created by cypress trees.

5.2-mile-long Lower Wekiva Loop Trail, then passes the northern trailhead. Continue north on the Florida Trail. Shortly before the end of the walk you'll pass a place called Dead Cow Sink, a depression in the ground with only a few scattered cow bones. At one time it probably contained the entire skeleton. Time and tourists have made the site's name almost meaningless. You'll find a large campground waiting at the northern terminus. And, unless you've arranged for a shuttle or a pickup, you'll need to retrace your steps.

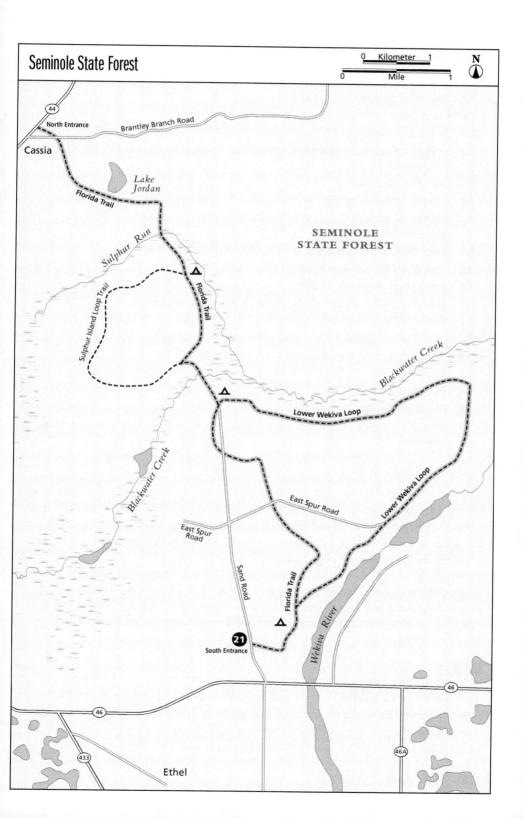

Seminole State Forest

Miles and Directions

The following directions are south to north.

0.0 Start at the trailhead at the parking lot kiosk.

0.4 Reach junction with a footpath. Follow the orange-blazed FNST.

0.7 Pass a shelter and large tent camping area.

0.8 Intersect the southern end of white-blazed 10.6-mile Lower Wekiva Loop Trail. Stay left on the orange-blazed trail.

2.0 Cross East Spur Road.

3.0 Cross the graded Sand Road.

3.6 Intersect the northern end of the white-blazed Lower Wekiva Loop Trail. Stay left on the orange-blazed trail.

3.7 Reach the blue-blazed side trail to Blackwater Creek campsite (500 feet).

3.8 Cross Blackwater Creek on a bridge.

4.0 Pass a horse trough with a pump.

4.1 Reach the junction of Sand and Grade Roads. Turn right onto Grade Road.

4.8 Cross Pine Road.

5.1 Cross Pine Road again. Arrive at Shark Tooth Springs campsite.

5.8 Reach junction with Palatka Road. Go right to follow Sand Road.

5.9 Join Atula Road.

7.3 Pass through a fence.

7.4 Pass Dead Cow Sink.

7.5 Arrive at a parking lot and kiosks. Unless you've arranged for a shuttle or a pickup, retrace your steps.

Lower Wekiva Loop Trail

The Lower Wekiva River State Preserve adjoins the state forest, but the main hike through it begins in the state forest, not the preserve. A hiking path at the entrance of the nearby reserve is much shorter and less interesting than this 9.7-mile linear and loop trail, a distance that includes the access/return walk from Seminole Forest's southern trailhead and the loop walk itself.

Finding the trailhead: The trailhead is located off State Road 46 in the forest's south parking area. Go through the walk-through gate and follow the orange blaze of the main FNST for 0.8 mile to the first campsite. The path will Y just after the campsite. Turn right to join the white-blazed Lower Wekiva Trail.

The Hike

The white-blazed Wekiva loop itself is 5.2 miles but you have to walk for almost a mile from south to north on the FNST to access it. The loop walk ends as it rejoins the main FNST just south of Blackwater Creek. The return from there to the south parking lot via the FNST is 3.6 miles. The Wekiva loop trail parallels meandering

Blackwater Creek for a good deal of the way. A primitive campsite is located at the walk's midpoint. It's actually possible to see bears on this walk; they've been spotted meandering along the trail itself. This very scenic hike is highly recommended.

Miles and Directions

0.0 Depart south parking lot, joining main FNST.

0.7 Reach first campsite. Go straight.

0.9 Trail Ys. Go right to join white-blazed Lower Wekiva Trail.

6.1 Rejoin main FNST orange-blazed trail. Go south (turn left).

8.8 Reach southern trailhead for Lower Wekiva Trail, on the left. Go straight.

9.7 Arrive back at south parking lot.

More Information

Local Information

Lake County Visitor Information: www.lakegovernment.com/visitors.

Local Events/Attractions

Much more hiking is available within the state forest, such as the 3.7-mile Sulphur Island Loop. Also, Rock Springs Run, another state park, is located near the forest entrance. Although there are hiking trails located here, none of them access Rock Springs Run or any other body of water. Hiking access to Rock Springs Run actually is through Wekiwa Springs State Park.

Lodging

Eustis, Lake County Visitor Information: www.lakegovernment.com/visitors.

Sanford, Seminole County Convention and Visitors Bureau: www.visitseminole.com/tourism-cvb.

Camping

Five primitive campsites are available for through hikers along the Florida National Scenic Trail. In addition, three primitive sites with fire rings and picnic tables are available by reservation; these also require a user fee. The Moccasin Springs Camp, located on the banks of Blackwater Creek, can accommodate only five persons. Oaks and Jumper Camps can hold up to twenty persons each.

Organizations

State Forests in Florida: www.fl-dof.com/state_forests/index.html.

Black bears are common in Central Florida, particularly at Wekiwa Springs State Park. Overnight campers must take special precautions to bear-proof their supplies.

Wekiwa Springs State Park is a 7,800-acre scenic wonder little changed from the days when the Timucuan Indians speared fish in the spring-fed creeks and stalked deer in the uplands. As the metropolitan Orlando area grows ever denser, Wekiwa Springs is turning into a priceless urban preserve of nature. It features extensive hiking with primitive wilderness camping in an otherwise heavily developed part of central Florida. The nearest town is Apopka, an Indian word apparently meaning "Big Potato."

Nearest town: Apopka
Start: Sand Lake parking lot
Distance: 10.2-mile loop
Approximate hiking time: 5 to 6 hours
Difficulty: Easy to moderate
Trail surface: Mostly dirt path
Seasons: Fall through spring
Other trail users: Nature watchers
Canine compatibility: Leashed dogs permitted
Land status: State park
Fees and permits: Entrance fee under $5

Schedule: Open 8:00 a.m. to sunset daily
Maps: Available at the ranger station
Trail contact: Wekiwa Springs State Park, 1800 Wekiwa Circle, Apopka, FL 32712; (407) 884-2008; www.floridastateparks.org/wekiwasprings. *Note:* Streets are known both as Wekiwa (name of the state park) and Wekiva (name of the river running through the park). If that seems confusing to you, residents don't know what to make of it either.

Finding the trailhead: The park is located about 20 minutes from Orlando. Turn off Interstate 4 at exit 94 and turn left to go under the State Road 436 overpass. Follow the signs on State Road 434 west to Wekiwa Springs Road. Turn right onto Wekiwa Springs Road and travel approximately 4 miles to the park entrance on the right. Turn left when the entrance road Ts after the ranger station. Follow the road until it ends at the Sand Lake parking lot. **GPS:** N28 43.423' W081 28.398'

The Hike

Traffic passing the entrance is so thick it almost demands a stoplight in order to drive out. Yet inside Wekiwa, it's back to the Florida of wading birds, otters, raccoons, alligators, and even black bears.

On weekends Sand Lake tends to attract a boisterous crowd, but a few hundred yards into the woods, the blaring boom box music will be filtered out. This loop trail soon moves among towering pines, thick palmettos, and a dense ground covering of ferns. If it weren't for the palmettos, it would be easy to mistake this for the pinewoods of a more northern state.

▶ Why do the spring and river have different but such similar names, an endless source of confusion? Both are Creek Indian words. Wekiwa means "spring of water"; Wekiva translates as "flowing water." Therefore, Wekiwa relates to everything in the park itself, where the spring originates, while Wekiva refers to the river.

Wildlife here is abundant, so don't be surprised to hear bushes moving or dead palm fronds snapping. White-tailed deer and black bear are common in the region, but the racket is probably nothing more than an armadillo.

The trail itself can be muddy after heavy rains. At the Sand Lake trailhead, go north, which will take you to some of most interesting parts of the walk and also offer you the opportunity to cut the hike short after 6.7 miles via a cross trail. You're not likely to bail out unless the weather has turned sour or the humidity is overwhelming. The scenery is just too pretty.

Moving forward, you'll quickly come to a primitive campsite at a spot called Camp Cozy. It is, too, with a chance to take fresh water from the crystal clear Rock

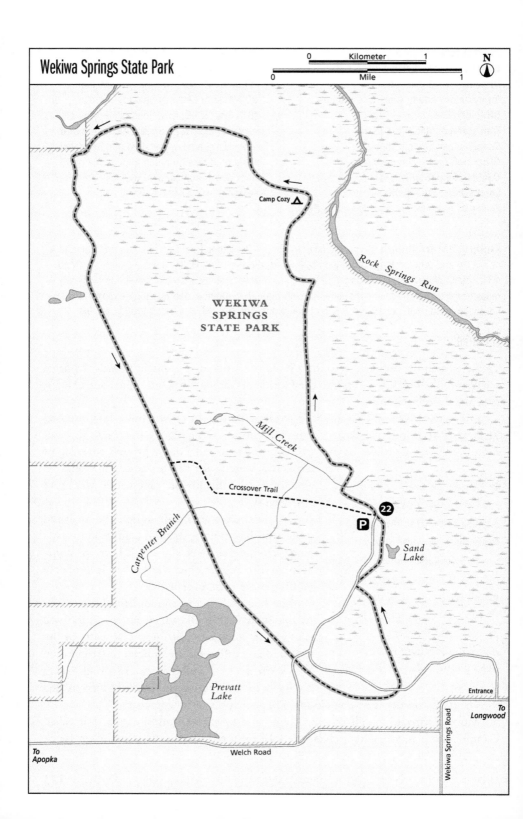

Wekiwa Springs State Park

0   Kilometer   1

0   Mile   1

N

Camp Cozy

Rock Springs Run

WEKIWA SPRINGS STATE PARK

Mill Creek

Crossover Trail

Carpenter Branch

22

P

Sand Lake

Prevatt Lake

Entrance

To Longwood

Wekiwa Springs Road

To Apopka

Welch Road

Springs Run, perhaps even take a dip in it. Enjoy this closeness to the fast stream since the hike will shortly move well away from it.

After passing the bailout cross trail at 6.7 miles, you'll encounter a large dry sinkhole to the east (left) of the trail. It's large enough to be a small and deep (for Florida) pond, but the water table is too low for the depression to fill. That doesn't mean conditions will change, since Florida's terrain is constantly changing due to the appearance of new sinkholes and the steady erosion of the limestone rock under most of the state. These Florida "earthquakes" usually occur on a small, individualized basis, sometimes swallowing up houses or taking big bites out of roadways.

Florida's largest sinkhole occurred here in 1981 when in one day the earth suddenly opened up in the town of Winter Park. Within 24 hours the sinkhole swallowed a house, public pool, and almost an entire city block, including some expensive sports cars from a helpless dealership. The shore of the sinkhole was stabilized and landscaped so the sinkhole now appears like a small lake. Yet the ground could open up again sometime to increase the lake's diameter.

Near the end of the hike you'll encounter a short 0.9-mile side trail on the right leading to Wekiva Springs itself, a wonderful place to take a dip if it's been a hot day. The spring basin is shallow, varying from 1 to 4 feet with a sandy bottom. If you brought a picnic lunch, a lawn chair, or a blanket for simply relaxing in the sun, the hillside overlooking the spring basin is where you want to head afterwards. Or, if you're still full of energy, rent a canoe to paddle the Wekiva River.

From this side trail to Wekiwa Springs, it's only another 1.2 miles to the parking lot at Sand Lake, the trail's end.

Miles and Directions

0.0 Start at the trailhead at Sand Lake parking area.

0.6 Cross an old railroad grade.

1.6 Cross the old railroad grade again.

2.6 Pass a primitive campsite.

4.3 Reach junction with a mountain biking trail.

6.7 Intersect a yellow-blazed trail. (**Option:** Turn left onto the yellow-blazed trail for a shorter loop.)

8.8 Pass a developed campground with water (fee).

9.0 Junction with 0.9-mile side trail on right to Wekiwa Springs. Cross paved park road.

9.6 Cross stream on a footbridge.

10.0 Water and restrooms available.

10.2 Arrive back at the Sand Lake parking lot.

Option: A shorter loop, the 5.3-mile Volksmarch Trail, begins near the spring boil. Information and a map are available at the ranger station.

More Information

Local Information

City of Apopka: www.apopka.net.

Local Events/Attractions

Wekiwa Park's main attraction is a bubbling clear spring that forms a huge natural swimming pool with a shallow sandy bottom, ideal for snorkeling (no diving permitted). On weekends, picnickers often fill the grassy bank overlooking the spring, spreading out beach blankets and lounge chairs. For a picnic in the shade, choose one of the nearby covered pavilions.

Wekiwa Springs sends 42 million gallons daily into the Wekiva River, an Outstanding Florida Waterway and one of Florida's most popular canoe trails. The gentle current provides a deceptively relaxing float downriver. Too far downstream, however, you could find the return against the current a real challenge. It's easier to paddle up the Wekiva River and then drift back to Wekiwa Springs Park. Canoe rentals are available inside the park.

Thirty- to sixty-minute Saturday Interpretive Programs are held at the campground amphitheater beginning at 10:00 a.m.

Lodging

Lodging is available at Apopka and Orlando.

Camping

To ensure that primitive sites don't become overcrowded, backpackers must check in at the entrance station like regular campers. There are also sixty developed campsites in the park. Reservations: (800) 326-3521; www.reserveamerica.com/index.jsp.

Organizations

Florida Department of Environmental Protection, Division of Recreation and Parks: www.dep .state.fl.us.

23 Tosohatchee Wildlife Management Area: Florida Trail Segment

At Tosohatchee WMA, man-made sounds disturb wildlife in the forest, which contains some of Central Florida's finest remaining cypress trees.

The 31,000-acre Tosohatchee Wildlife Management Area borders 19 miles of the St. Johns River. Its landscape is a showcase of how plant communities are shaped by the alternating cycles of flood and fire that create a patchwork of swamps, marshes, hammocks, and pine flatwoods. The WMA contains one of the finest stands of virgin cypress remaining in North America. Pronounced tos-uh-HATCH-ee, the word is actually a simplification of the Indian term Tootoosahatchee, meaning either "chicken creek" or "fowl creek." You'll be seeing some of that creek on the hike here, an excellent trail for overnight backpacking trips. Tosohatchee has almost 60 miles of hiking trails, including a through section of the Florida National Scenic Trail (FNST). The featured hike is an out-and-back on the FNST to a primitive campsite.

Nearest town: Christmas
Start: Parking area on Powerline Road
Distance: 4.6 miles out and back
Approximate hiking time: 3 hours or overnight

Difficulty: Easy to moderate, depending on rains
Trail surface: Dirt path
Seasons: Fall through spring
Other trail users: Hunters in season

Canine compatibility: Leashed dogs permitted on the trail but not at primitive campsites; in effect, no pets on overnight hikes

Land status: Florida Wildlife Management Area

Fees and permits: Daily use fee under $5; primitive camping fee under $5. One ax or hatchet is permitted per campsite; no machetes. Use only dead, downed wood for fires.

Schedule: Open 8:00 a.m. to sunset. Frequent hunts begin in September and last through March. Check the schedule at http://myfwc .com/recreation/tosohatchee/whentovisit.asp

Maps: Available at the park office or online at http://myfwc.com/recreation/tosohatchee/visitorinfo.asp

Trail contact: Tosohatchee WMA, 3365 Taylor Creek Road, Christmas, FL 32709; (407) 568-5893; http://myfwc.com/recreation/tosohatchee/visitorinfo.asp

Special considerations: This is a public hunting area. During hunts, hikers should wear 500 square inches of blaze-orange clothing above the waist, and it must be visible in both front and back. Hunting schedule is available at www.myfwc.com/hunting.

Jurisdiction is changing from the Park Service to Fish and Wildlife Conservation Commission, which promotes hunting over hiking. This trail used to have two primitive campsites and now has only one. Anticipate that more changes may have occurred; check before your visit.

Finding the trailhead: From Orlando, travel east on State Road 50. Turn right onto Taylor Creek Road and go 3 miles to the WMA entrance on the left. From State Road 528 (Beeline Expressway), take the State Road 520 exit and go north on SR 520 approximately 0.5 mile. Turn right onto Taylor Creek Road and proceed approximately 2 miles to the WMA entrance on the right.

There are two trails leading to the Tiger Branch camping area. (*Note:* The one at Sabal Palm, still identified on many maps, has been closed.) The longer trail begins on Powerline Road. From the entrance kiosk take Beehead Road to St. Nicholas Road and turn left. You'll shortly turn right onto Powerline Road; about 5 miles from the entrance is a small parking area. (The larger parking lots on the left you pass before the trailhead are for equestrian trails.) A small sign on the right designates the Swamp Spur Trail. From this point, Tiger Branch is 2.3 miles. A shorter trail begins at the end of Beehead Road, 3 miles from the entrance. From Beehead Road it's only 1.8 miles to Tiger Branch and 0.8 mile to Jim Creek along the Swamp Spur Trail. **GPS:** N28 29.910' W080 59.805'

The Hike

The section of Florida Trail passing through the WMA is blazed in the usual orange.

To reach the trailhead along Powerline Road, drive along a dike road that passes through scores of power line transmission poles. When dry, the walk encompasses mostly level terrain, an easy stroll through a pine forest that gives way to a lower swampy area full of serenading frogs. Wooden logs are provided as footbridges across some streams. Pay attention to the water markers if you start from Powerline Road. During high-water periods, wading may be necessary.

Wildlife here include numerous wading and shore birds, deer, snakes, armadillos, bobcats, turkeys, gray foxes, hawks, owls, the Florida black

▶ At over 200 feet, the alligator at Jungle Adventures theme park, close to the Tosohatchee Wildlife Management Area, is considered the largest nonorganic alligator in the world. Jungle Adventures is also one of Florida's largest alligator farms.

Tosohatchee Wildlife Management Area

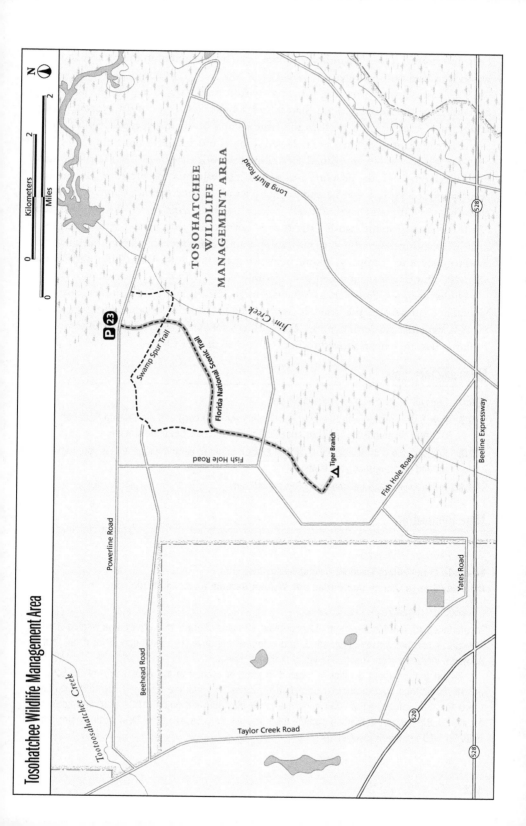

bear, and ospreys. Florida panther sightings have been claimed in the refuge, and bald eagles nest undisturbed here.

This vast management area contains a virgin pine flatwoods (one of only a few remaining in the entire United States) and a huge 900-acre virgin cypress swamp (along Jim Creek). This is perhaps the largest stand of uncut cypress left in the state. Some of the giant slash pines are believed to be as much as 250 years old.

The reason this area remained so well preserved is that from 1930 until the state purchased it in 1977, the property was used as a private hunting preserve. The hunters went to great lengths to create and maintain an ideal game habitat. Hunts were fewer than fifty days annually and included archery, muzzle-loading gun, and modern gun. With the management transfer, the fear is that the hunting period will increase—a curious situation, since the state justified spending millions of dollars to purchase the land to open it to "camping, hiking, picnicking, fishing, horseback riding, and natural scenery." Hunting was supposed to be prohibited.

Under even the Park Service's management, the hiking trail has undergone considerable changes over the years. It once passed the Beehead Ranch House, a classic Florida structure made of cypress and palm logs formerly used by the hunt club. The building has since been moved to Fort Christmas, nearer Orlando.

Miles and Directions

0.0 Start at the trailhead off Powerline Road.

0.5 Reach the junction with Beehead Road (alternate trailhead) and the Swamp Spur Trail. The 0.8-mile Swamp Spur Trail goes left (east) to Taylor Creek. Continue straight.

2.3 Intersect the 0.1-mile side trail to Tiger Branch primitive camping area. This is your turn-around point; retrace your steps.

4.6 Arrive back at the trailhead and Powerline Road.

More Information

Local Information
Titusville Area Visitors Council: www.spacecityflusa.com.
Orlando/Orange County Convention and Visitors Bureau: www.orlandoinfo.com.

Local Events/Attractions
Tosohatchee Wildlife Management Area contains 19 miles of roads that offer prime wildlife viewing. However, some are mostly sugar sand, and a four-wheel drive is recommended for a full tour. In addition, there are more than 20 miles of multiuse trails.

A loop trail of about 3 miles is located in another section of the park, south of SR 520. It's a very scenic loop hike to another part of Taylor Creek. To reach the trailhead, turn left onto Taylor Creek Road as you leave the WMA and drive to SR 520. Turn left onto SR 520 and drive southeast for almost 8 miles to the marked parking area. You will be paralleling the FNST at this point, which uses SR 520 to access Tosohatchee.

Canaveral National Seashore (321-867-4077; www.nps.gov/cana) adjoins the Merritt Island National Wildlife Refuge east of Titusville. The seashore has 25 miles of unbroken beach.

The Kennedy Space Center offers public tours. For shuttle launch schedules, log onto www .nasa.gov/centers/kennedy/home/index.html.

Lodging

Lodging is available in Titusville.

Titusville Area Visitors Council: www.spacecityflusa.com.

Orlando/Orange County Convention and Visitors Bureau: www.orlandoinfo.com.

Camping

The one primitive campsite in the WMA can be reached only by trekking in. Reservations must be made at least two weeks in advance by calling (407) 568-5893. No camping is permitted the night before or during quota hunts.

Organizations

Florida Fish and Wildlife Conservation Commission: http://myfwc.com.

An aquatic plant, the alligator flag gets its name from the fact it thrives in wet places that alligators typically inhabit.

This easy walk makes a nice, short stop for those traveling on Florida's west coast. The Little Manatee River divides the 2,400-acre park into two sections. The southern part, with its developed campground, horse trail, and canoe launch, is what most people see. That's because the northern half is open only to controlled foot traffic. Hikers must stop at the ranger station (open at 8:00 a.m.) to get the lock combination to enter the parking area at the trailhead. This leg of the Florida National Scenic Trail is considered the finest hiking for miles around. But during the summer rains, it can be extremely wet, so check ahead.

Nearest town: Wimauma
Start: Hiking trail parking area north of the main park entrance
Distance: 6.3-mile loop
Approximate hiking time: 2 to 3 hours
Difficulty: Easy
Trail surface: Dirt footpath, boardwalk, bridges
Seasons: Fall through spring
Other trail users: Hikers only in this area
Canine compatibility: Leashed pets permitted;
pets allowed in the campground
Land status: State park
Fees and permits: Park admission fee under $5
Schedule: Open 8:00 a.m. to sunset; must check at park office for access
Maps: Available at the park office
Trail contact: Little Manatee River State Park, 215 Lightfoot Road, Wimauma, FL 33598; (813) 671-5005; www.floridastateparks.org/littlemanateeriver

Finding the trailhead: Coming south from Tampa via Interstate 75: take exit 240A (Sun City exit) and go east on Sun City Center Boulevard to U.S. Highway 301. Turn right onto US 301 and go south 4 miles. Turn right onto Lightfoot Road and go 0.7 mile to Sundance Trail and turn right. The park entrance will be on the left in 0.5 mile. Look for the entrance signs.

Going north from Sarasota Bradenton on I-75: Take exit 229 and go east to US 301. Turn right and go north 6 miles, then turn left onto Lightfoot Road. Go 0.7 mile to Sundance Trail and turn right. The park entrance will be on the left in 0.5 mile. Look for the entrance signs.

The hiking trailhead is located in the park's northern wilderness area on US 301, 3 miles north of the park entrance. You must sign in before hiking in order to obtain the trailhead parking area lock combination. **GPS:** N27 40.506' W082 20.921'

The Hike

A short access trail leads to the 6.4-mile loop, which is blazed in orange. The side trail to the campground (Mile 3.3 going counterclockwise) is blazed in blue. Much of the trail meanders through sand pine, palmetto, and oak hammocks. Wild azaleas along the trail make this a colorful route in February and March. Since human intrusion here is limited, hikers have a good chance of glimpsing the resident white-tailed deer, turkeys, foxes, bobcats, or scrub jays.

The terrain is flat for easy walking, but a lot of effort went into building this pathway: There are two boardwalks and almost twenty bridges. You will also become familiar with picturesque Cypress Creek flowing in from the north, whose flood plain tends to dominate the northern corridor of the walk, mostly in a very scenic way. The shallow tea-colored stream normally is unable to hide its rippled sand bottom.

▶ The Little Manatee River, designated an Outstanding Florida Water, flows almost 40 miles before emptying into Tampa Bay. About 4.5 miles of the river runs through Little Manatee River State Park.

After heavy rains and the creek floods, you may never witness that tranquil scene. Reaching 2.3 miles, you'll find the side trail to the trail's single primitive campsite, which also has picnic tables for day hikers. Continuing on the main trail, the hike will soon curve left (south) toward the Little Manatee River, which borders almost a third of the entire walk. You'll be walking along bluffs over the Little Manatee River, encounter where Cypress Creek flows into it, and use a number of bridges to return to the trailhead at 6.4 miles.

Little Manatee River State Park

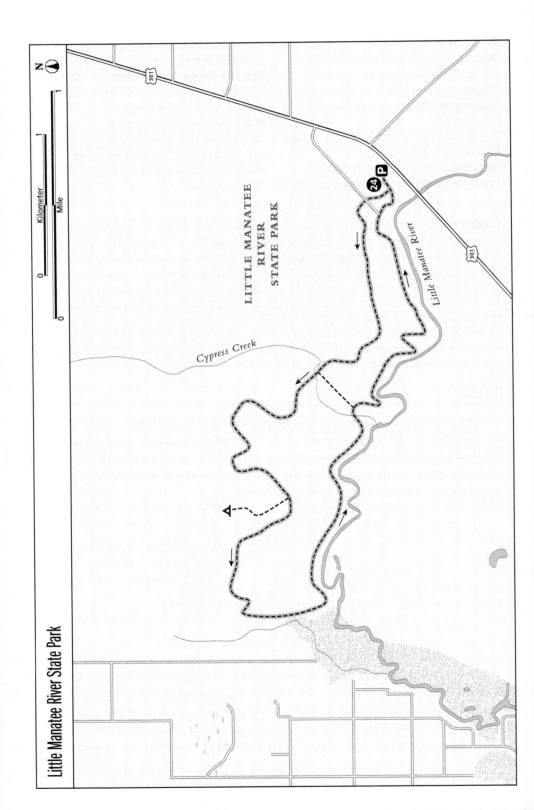

LITTLE MANATEE
RIVER
STATE PARK

Cypress Creek

Little Manatee River

301

Miles and Directions

0.0 Start at the trailhead in the hiking parking lot, 3 miles north of the main park entrance.

0.1 The short access trail joins the main loop trail, which you'll follow in a counterclockwise direction.

1.5 Reach the northern junction with a 0.2-mile cross trail that leads to Little Manatee River. Go straight.

1.7 Cross bridge at Cypress Creek.

2.3 Pass junction with a 0.2-mile trail to primitive campground. Trail will soon gradually turn south (left).

3.6 View from bluff above Little Manatee River.

4.7 Southern end of cross trail.

5.0 Reach the southern junction of 0.2-mile cross trail leading north. Go straight.

5.6 Enjoy view from a river bluff. Continue straight.

6.3 Turn right at junction onto the access trail.

6.4 Arrive back at the hiking parking lot.

More Information

Local Information

Manatee County, the Bradenton Area Convention and Visitors Bureau: www.floridaislandbeaches .org.

Local Events/Attractions

No swimming is allowed in the park, but canoeing and kayaking are popular activities.
  The main park also has nature trails for easier walks.

Lodging

Lodging is available in Bradenton: www.floridaislandbeaches.org.

Camping

The developed campground at the park has 34 campsites, plus the trail has a primitive site that must be reserved in advance. Reservations: (800) 326-3521; www.reserveamerica.com/index.jsp.

Organizations

Florida Department of Environmental Protection, Division of Recreation and Parks: www.dep .state.fl.us/parks.

25 Lake Kissimmee State Park: North and Buster Island Loop Trails

The tall gray sandhill crane with its distinctive red head is a common sight at Lake Kissimmee State Park.

Depending on your interests, trail hiking may become secondary in this 5,930-acre park. Fishermen will enjoy Lake Kissimmee, rated one of the top largemouth bass waters in the entire country. Numerous high-money fishing tournaments have been held on the lake. A boat ramp is available in the park. Fishing is typically best March through May but can be quite productive year-round. A Florida fishing license is required.

With more than 200 bird species, Lake Kissimmee State Park is one of central Florida's best birding areas, offering the rare opportunity to see bald eagles, snail kites, and even whooping cranes. The park is also home to fifty species of plants and animals regarded as threatened, of special concern, or endangered. But best known of all is the park's 1876-era cow camp, a living history exhibit with the chance to talk with an old-style Florida cow hunter who used a whip to herd his cattle, leading to the famous term "Florida cracker" that refers to the sound made by the whip.

Nearest town: Hesperides
Start: Trailhead at west end of parking lot
Distance: North Loop Trail, 6.3-mile loop; Buster Island Loop, 6.5-mile loop
Approximate hiking time: 2 to 3 hours per hike
Difficulty: Easy
Trail surface: Mostly dirt path
Seasons: Fall through early spring
Other trail users: Fishermen, nature watchers

Canine compatibility: Leashed pets permitted
Land status: State park
Fees and permits: Park admission fee under $5
Schedule: Open 8:00 a.m. to sunset
Maps: Available at the ranger station
Trail contact: Lake Kissimmee State Park, 14248 Camp Mack Road, Lake Wales, FL 33853; (863) 696-1112; www.floridastateparks.org/lakekissimmee

Finding the trailhead: From U.S. Highway 27/Lake Wales, travel east for 15 miles on State Road 60. Turn left (north) onto Boy Scout Road to Camp Mack Road. Turn right onto Camp Mack Road and go 5.5 miles to park main entrance.

From Interstate 95 on the Atlantic coast, take exit 147 and go west on SR 60. (If you're traveling the Florida Turnpike, a toll road, take exit 163 at Yeehaw Junction and go west on SR 60.) Continue west on SR 60, crossing the Kissimmee River and passing the River Ranch Resort. Turn right (north) onto Boy Scout Road to Camp Mack Road. Turn right onto Camp Mack Road and go 5.5 miles to park main entrance.

Take the park's main road to the parking area located between the two loop trails. A blue-blazed 0.3-mile access path at the west end of the parking area leads to the loops. **GPS:** N27 56.534' W081 21.230'

The Hikes

The two loop trails, the North Loop and the Buster Island Loop, are just under 6 miles each and traverse floodplains that may be inundated by summer rains. The main trails are blazed in white, connecting trails in blue.

At least fifty animal species considered endangered, threatened, rare, or of special concern live in this park. Some of the more common animals to watch for are white-tailed deer, sandhill cranes, bobcats, turkeys, and bald eagles.

On the North Loop going clockwise, you'll pass a turpentine workers' cemetery that dates back to 1912. Also watch for a blue-blazed side trail to Gobbler Ridge, an elevated area said to have been created by high waves off Lake Kissimmee. It now contains an abundance of live oak. The Buster Island Loop tends toward higher ground and features a hardwood hammock.

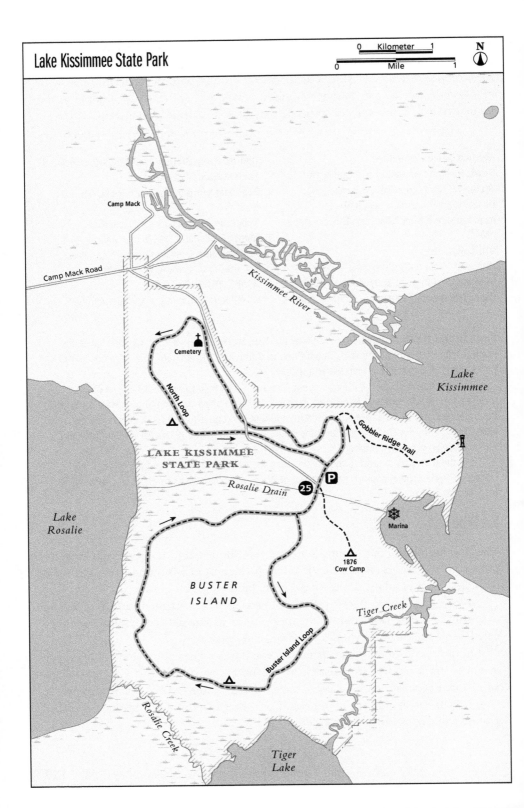

Lake Kissimmee State Park

Afterward, plan on spending at least an hour at the 1876 "Cow Camp," which is staffed by park rangers from 9:30 a.m. to 4:30 p.m. weekends and holidays only. Florida has been one of the top-five cattle states for decades. Here more than 200 acres are reserved for raising a herd of scrub cows and horses, just as Florida "crackers" did in the 1800s.

The Cow Camp consists of a corral for livestock and a wooden lean-to that a cracker would have lived in. A ranger explains what life was like and demonstrates some of the skills needed back then, including a little of the whip-cracking that old-time wranglers used to move the herds.

▶ Florida cowpokes were known as "crackers" because of the whips they used to move cattle.

The Cow Camp is not on the main hiking trail. It has a short pathway of its own from a side road. Signs point the way.

North Loop Trail

Miles and Directions

0.0 Start at west end of the parking lot.
0.3 The access trail joins the North Loop Trail; go right.
0.4 Cross a park road.
0.8 Pass the junction with the blue-blazed 1.4-mile side trail to Gobbler Ridge.
1.3 Cross a park road.
2.1 Cross a park road.
3.2 Pass the turpentine workers' cemetery.
3.7 Cross a park road.
4.5 Pass a campsite.
6.0 Reach the junction with the parking lot access trail; go right.
6.3 Arrive back at the parking lot.

Buster Island Loop

Miles and Directions

0.0 Start at the marked trailhead at the western end of the parking lot.
0.3 The access trail joins the Buster Island Loop. Go left.
3.7 Pass the Buster Island campsite.
4.6 Traverse an oak hammock.
5.5 Cross an old barbed-wire fenceline.
6.2 Return to the junction with the access trail; go left.
6.5 Arrive back at the parking lot.

More Information

Local Information

Polk County Convention and Visitors Bureau: www.sunsational.org.

Local Events/Attractions

An 1876 "Cow Camp" demonstrates living conditions of the time. The camp is open only on weekends and holidays from 9:30 a.m. to 4:30 p.m.

Guided overnight backpacking trips are available starting each year in November. Call for dates and times: (863) 696-1112.

Guided bird walks are held on selected Saturdays from October to March. Call (863) 696-1112 for details.

Lodging

Lakes Wales: www.sunsational.org.

Camping

There's a primitive campsite on each trail, as well as a public campground with 60 developed sites. Reservations: (800) 326-3521; www.reserveamerica.com/index.jsp.

Organizations

Florida Department of Environmental Protection, Division of Recreation and Parks: www.dep .state.fl.us/parks.

Long Haulers

Trees knocked over by windstorms are not always immediately cleared. This tree has been down for several years.

The 389,000-acre Ocala National Forest was the first designated national forest east of the Mississippi River. The Big Scrub, as it is affectionately known, is the world's largest stand of sand pine scrub forest. It also contains one of the most scenic extensions of the Florida National Scenic Trail, a 75-mile leg that's considered the "crown jewel" of the system.

Divided into two main sections, north and south, the trail passes through rolling hills and longleaf pine forests, skirts as many as sixty ponds, and ventures into numerous cypress and gum swamps. Hikers usually don't need to worry about soaked feet in the swamps—many of the wet spots are spanned by boardwalks.

Nearest town: Palatka
Start: Buckman Lock
Distance: 34.0 miles one-way
Approximate hiking time: 2 to 3 days
Difficulty: Easy to moderate
Trail surface: Dirt path, forest roads
Seasons: Fall through spring

Other trail users: Some areas of forest roads shared by ATVs, trucks, equestrians
Canine compatibility: Leashed dogs permitted
Land status: National forest
Fees and permits: No fees or permits required for through hiking. Day-use fees at Juniper Springs, Silver Glen Springs, Wildcat Lake,

Clearwater Lake, and Alexander Springs Recreation Areas. Annual passes available for Juniper Springs, Silver Glen Springs, Wildcat Lake, Alexander Springs, and Clearwater Lake. Fee schedule is available at www.fs.fed.us/r8/florida/passes.

Schedule: Forest open 24 hours a day; hunting season mid-November to mid-January, with some restrictions for other users. Lock at the northern end is closed Wednesday.

Maps: Available from Forest Service office and the Florida Trail Association

Trail contacts: Lake George District, 17147 East Highway 40, Silver Springs, FL 34488; (352) 625-2520; open weekdays only 7:30 a.m. to 4:00 p.m.

Seminole Ranger District, 40929 State Road 19, Umatilla, FL 32784; (352) 669-3153; open weekdays only 7:30 a.m. to 4:30 p.m.

Visitor centers in Silver Springs, Salt Springs, and Altoona open daily 9:00 a.m. to 5:00 p.m. except holidays; www.fs.fed.us/r8/florida/recreation/index_oca.shtml.

Special considerations: If you intend to camp in the forest, be aware this is prime black bear habitat. The bears are interested in your food, not you. Don't leave anything out overnight that isn't sealed.

This is also a public hunting area. During hunting season, hikers should wear 500 square inches of blaze-orange clothing above the waist, and it must be visible in both front and back. Hunting schedule available at www.myfwc.com/hunting.

Finding the trailhead: Take State Road 19 about 8 miles south of the town of Palatka. Look for a side road that leads to Buckman Lock, part of the old Florida Barge Canal. Parking is available. Gates on both sides of the canal are unlocked only during specific hours, presently 9:00 a.m. to 5:00 p.m. daily. Call the lock attendant at (386) 329-3575 for current schedule or the Rodman Campground at (386) 326-2847. **GPS:** N28 58.620' W081 33.011'

The Hike

This hike can be broken into several easy day-hike sections, so don't feel that you have to tackle this entire route in one trek.

Hikers may need to use a whistle to attract the attendant's attention at Buckman Lock. At about Mile 7 the trail arrives at the spillway of Rodman Dam, built as part of the barge canal project. Environmentalists want to remove the dam so that the Ocklawaha River can be returned to its natural state. In the meantime, the spillway is a popular place to fish and camp.

Going south, you almost immediately come upon a primitive camping area at Caravelle Ranch. You'll pass the entrance of the Rodman Campground with more developed sites at Mile 5. Continuing south, the trail crosses Forest Roads 77, 31, 88, and 75 and then reaches the shores of Lake Delancy (Mile 14), a good spot for water and camping. Another campsite is at Grassy Pond (Mile 18).

▶ The USDA Forest Service and the U.S. Navy have an agreement for use of the Pinecastle bombing range. The Navy has used the range, established by the Army Air Corps in 1943, for training since the 1950s.

From Grassy Pond the trail crosses FR 88, County Road 316, County Road 318, FR 88 again, and then Forest Road 51. Shortly after Mile

30 is a junction with a 3-mile side trail leading to the Salt Springs Recreation Area, which has complete facilities and swimming pool–like natural springs.

Back on the main trail, continue across Forest Roads 90 and 65 to Hopkins Prairie, which offers complete facilities and lakeside camping at Mile 35.

Miles and Directions

The following milepoints are traveled north to south.

0.0 Start at Buckman Lock. (**FYI:** The lock is open 9:00 a.m. to 5:00 p.m. daily. Check in at the visitor center first.)

0.2 Pass Caravelle Ranch camping area.

2.0 Pass SR 19.

5.0 Pass Rodman Campground entrance station.

6.4 Cross the Rodman Spillway. (**FYI:** Spillway hours are 8:30 a.m. to 2:00 p.m.; closed Wednesday.)

7.3 Reach Rodman Reservoir. (**FYI:** Good lakeside camping is available here.)

8.8 Cross FR 77.

9.2 Cross Forest Road 31A.

13.7 Pass Lake Delancy Campground. (**FYI:** Water and latrines are available; no electricity.)

14.0 Cross Forest Road 85A.

14.3 Cross Forest Road 56.

17.7 Reach junction with blue-blazed trail coming from the right to Grassy Pond. (**Option:** Follow blue-blazed trail to lake camping.)

18.0 Cross Forest Road 88C.

18.7 Cross Forest Road 88-4.

19.4 Cross CR 316.

19.7 Reach junction with blue-blazed trail coming from the left. (**FYI:** The 0.4-mile side trail leads to a convenience store.)

20.3 Cross Forest Road 63.

20.6 Cross Forest Road 97A.

21.0 Reach a junction with two segments of the Florida National Scenic Trail (FNST), the eastern and western loops. (**FYI:** This hike describes the eastern loop.) Turn left.

21.5 Cross FR 63.

23.2 Cross Forest Road 50.

23.7 Cross Forest Road 19.

24.7 Cross paved County Road 314.

25.1 Cross FR 88.

26.7 Cross FR 50.

27.0 Cross FR 51.

27.8 Reach junction with blue-blazed trail coming from the left. (**FYI:** This 3.5-mile trail leads to Salt Springs Campground, a restaurant, and other niceties of civilization.)

29.0 Cross FR 90.

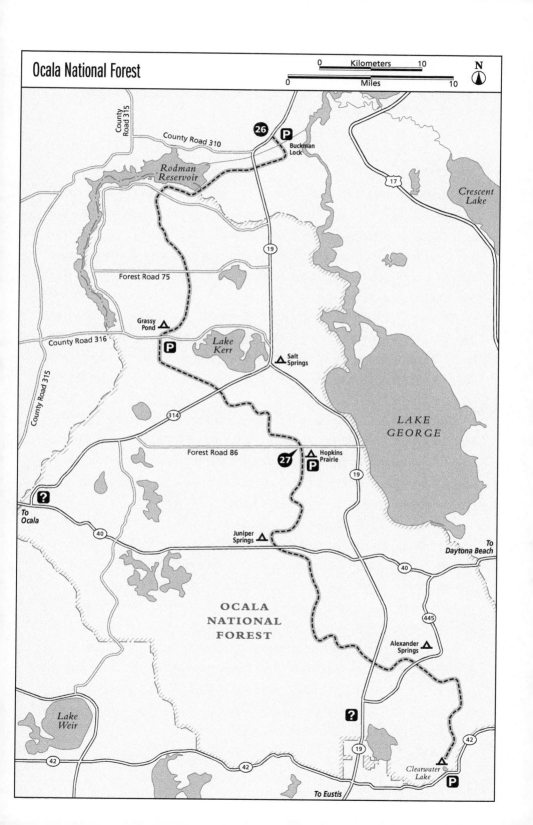

29.3 Cross FR 65.

30.0 Cross Forest Road 90A.

34.0 Arrive at junction with blue-blazed trail on the left to Hopkins Prairie developed camp-ground and the end of the Ocala North hike.

SINKHOLES

Earthquakes are one of the few violent natural forces that have not had a hand in shaping Florida. So, instead of concerns about the ground trembling, the people of Central and North Florida have a different worry: the ground could swallow them up. This uncommon but always annoying problem is created by sinkholes, giant maws in the ground that appear suddenly anytime, anywhere. In the past few years, they've opened under highways, apartment buildings, and in the middle of nowhere.

Florida's largest sinkhole, in the city of Winter Park near Orlando, claimed several expensive sports cars, a house, several trees, and a road before it stopped gobbling away the earth. Today, the sinkhole is filled with water, resembling a placid pond. Several roads that were eaten away are now dead-end instead of through streets. A large, hungry sinkhole can never be filled.

Sinkholes are a sobering reminder of the awesome power of the Floridan aquifer, the huge underground river that flows beneath much of the state. The aquifer normally flows dozens of feet below ground level. Rising water sometimes pushes it toward the surface, causing it to bulldoze away tons of soil, which often produces a cave-in. Typically, these cave-ins happen incredibly fast and without warning.

Sinkholes, however, can also be created by the rainwater needed to recharge the underground aquifer, one of the state's most important sources of fresh drinking water. When Florida was covered by sea water thousands of years ago, living organisms deposited thick layers of limestone on the ocean floor. After the water receded, this limestone became the state's land base. Rainwater slowly seeped into the limestone, dissolving it to form many small caves, hollows, and fissures.

Although rain water is quite pure to drink, the drops become slightly acidic as they absorb carbon dioxide both from the air and from decaying vegetation. The mild acid is able to eat away and dissolve Florida's limestone bedrock. Eventually, the ground surface may collapse, to form a sinkhole or a crater-like depression. Limestone terrain that has been shaped by both rain and groundwater is known as "karst."

More Information

Local Information

Ocala/Marion County Chamber of Commerce: www.ocalacc.com/ocala_florida/templates/tourism.aspx?articleid=16.

Local Events/Attractions

Ocala National Forest (www.fs.fed.us/r8/florida/recreation/index_oca.shtml) is an outdoor paradise. Scores of tiny lakes are hidden away in the forest, many of them ideal for fishing and primitive camping. Developed camping areas are located at Alexander Springs and Juniper Springs, two freshwater springs that double as natural swimming pools.

At Alexander Springs, the bottom slopes away to a depth of 30 feet near the middle, making it an ideal training ground for scuba diving classes. Fish life along the riverbank is prolific and easily accessible to snorkelers. Canoes can be rented from a concessionaire on the grounds.

Nearby Juniper Springs, which is much smaller, doesn't attract the same crowds as Alexander Springs because of the lack of diving and swimming opportunities. Juniper's spring boil, where the water gushes out of the ground, has been modernized into a huge concrete-lined swimming pool.

Lodging

Cabin rental is available at Lake Dorr and Sweetwater Springs. Contact Recreation Resource Management, Inc., 26701 East Highway 40, Silver Springs, FL 34488; (352) 625-0546.

Camping

Only tents are allowed in the general forest area. Motor homes, RVs, campers, trailers, and pop-ups are limited to designated areas. Log onto www.fs.fed.us/r8/florida/recreation/index_oca.shtml for a list of available locations. Detailed campsite descriptions are available at www.forestcamping.com/dow/southern/ocalcmp.htm, an excellent online guide to national forest camping throughout Florida.

Salt Springs Campground, Alexander Springs Recreation Area, Juniper Springs Recreation Area, and Clearwater Lake accept reservations (call 877-444-6777). The other developed campgrounds are available for a fee on a first-come, first-served basis. Firewood for campfires may be taken from dead and down trees without a permit.

Organizations

National Forests in Florida, 325 John Knox Road, Suite F-100, Tallahassee, FL 32303; (850) 523-8500; www.fs.fed.us/r8/florida/contact.

Pine trees and saw palmetto characterize much of the Florida Trail's southern section in the Ocala National Forest.

The Ocala South Trail traverses mostly pine and hardwood forests, offering one of Florida's drier hiking routes. It passes through Farles Prairie, a huge grassy expanse that's often an excellent place for spotting wildlife. You can increase your likelihood of spotting early-morning wildlife by camping here.

See map on page 144.
Nearest town: Salt Springs
Start: Hopkins Prairie Campground

Distance: 38.4 miles one-way
Approximate hiking time: 3 to 4 days
Difficulty: Easy to moderate

Trail surface: Dirt path, forest roads, boardwalks

Seasons: Fall through spring

Other trail users: ATVs, trucks, equestrians on some areas of forest roads

Canine compatibility: Leashed dogs permitted

Land status: National forest

Fees and permits: No fees or permits required for through hiking. Day-use fees required at Juniper Springs, Silver Glen Springs, Wildcat Lake, Clearwater Lake, and Alexander Springs Recreation Areas. Annual passes available for Juniper Springs, Silver Glen Springs, Wildcat Lake, Alexander Springs, and Clearwater Lake. Fee schedule is available at www.fs.fed.us/r8/florida/passes.

Schedule: Forest open 24 hours a day; hunting season mid-November to mid-January, with some restrictions for other users. Lock at the northern end is closed on Wednesday.

Maps: Available from Forest Service office and the Florida Trail Association

Trail contacts: Lake George District, 17147 East Highway 40, Silver Springs, FL 34488; (352) 625-2520; open weekdays only 7:30 a.m. to 4:00 p.m.

Seminole Ranger District, 40929 State Road 19, Umatilla, FL 32784; (352) 669-3153; open weekdays only 7:30 a.m. to 4:30 p.m.

Visitor centers in Silver Springs, Salt Springs, and Altoona open daily 9:00 a.m. to 5:00 p.m. except holidays; www.fs.fed.us/r8/florida/recreation/index_oca.shtml.

Special considerations: If you intend to camp in the forest, be aware this is prime black bear habitat. The bears are interested in your food, not in you. Don't leave anything out overnight that isn't sealed. This is also a public hunting area. During hunts, hikers should wear 500 square inches of blaze-orange clothing above the waist, and it must be visible in both front and back. Hunting schedule is available at www.myfwc.com/hunting.

Finding the trailhead: The developed campground at Hopkins Prairie is the preferred parking area. From Salt Springs take State Road 19 south 8.4 miles to Hopkins Prairie Road (Forest Road 86). Turn west onto Hopkins Prairie Road and go about 3 miles to Forest Road 86-F on the right. Turn right onto FR 86-F and go about 1 mile to the campground.

The Hike

This hike can be broken into several easy day-hike sections, so don't feel that you have to tackle the entire route in one trek.

From Hopkins Prairie the trail crosses FR 86 and then enters the Juniper Prairie Wilderness Area, where hunting is prohibited. Crossing Forest Roads 10 and 76, you arrive at Hidden Pond at Mile 5.7, with primitive sites and a chance to swim.

From here the trail crosses Whiskey and Whispering Creeks (you may have to wade during high water). It then skirts the south edge of Juniper Prairie and arrives at Juniper Springs Recreation Area (Mile 10.9), one of the two largest campgrounds in the forest. Leaving Juniper Springs Recreation Area, the trail crosses State Road 40 and then follows a boardwalk over a stretch of marshland. After crossing Forest Road 599, the trail arrives at Farles Prairie (Mile 17.5), a huge grassy expanse that's often an excellent place for spotting wildlife. Hikers can camp here on the northern end.

Crossing Forest Road 595, follow the blue-blazed trail (Mile 20.5) that goes 0.1 mile east to a campsite with water and latrines.

Continue 2 more miles to another blue-blazed side trail that loops around Buck Lake, one of Ocala's more popular "wilderness" campgrounds. The trail then crosses County Road 9277, SR 19, Forest Road 525, and State Road 445 to reach the blue-blazed 0.5-mile trail that leads to the Alexander Springs Recreation Area (Mile 28). Alexander Springs is a gorgeous freshwater spring with sand beach, well worth seeing. And very popular on most weekends.

Back on the main trail, follow a series of boardwalks—a long one before Forest Road 539 and several short ones through another swamp. At Mile 33.5 the trail cuts through a power line right-of-way, then follows a boardwalk over a creek. Cross Forest Road 538 and then a backwoods dirt road. Almost at the end of the hike, look for the Golden Blaze Tree, marked in 1986 to commemorate the Ocala Trail's first twenty years.

In a few hundred more yards, reach a 0.3-mile blue-blazed trail to Clearwater Lake Campground. Officially the Ocala Trail ends at County Road 42, just 0.3 mile east of the campground entrance. CR 42 also marks Ocala's southern boundary.

SCRUB JAYS

The scrub jay, a threatened species that is one of Florida's most interesting and attractive birds, is frequently sighted in Ocala National Forest. A member of the crow family, scrub jays are common throughout the southwestern United States; east of the Mississippi, they live only in Florida.

As the name implies, scrub jays live around the thickets of short bushy oaks known as scrub. They feed on acorns and, just like squirrels, sometimes bury the acorns for future use.

Scrub jays are wary when feeding. Normally one bird will act as a sentinel while the others eat. Yet scrub jays also become quite accustomed to people and often visit the most heavily used parts of the forest.

Miles and Directions

The following milepoints are traveled north to south.

0.0 Start at junction with blue-blazed trail to Hopkins Prairie Campground.

1.2 Cross FR 86.

2.2 Reach boundary of Juniper Prairie Wilderness Area. (**FYI:** Hunting is prohibited in the wilderness area.)

3.0 Cross FR 10.

5.7 Arrive at Hidden Pond. (**FYI:** Primitive camping and swimming are available here.)

6.8 Cross Whiskey Creek Bridge.

8.0 Cross Whispering Creek. (**FYI:** During high water, you may have to wade the creek.)

11.0 Reach Juniper Springs Recreation Area. (**FYI:** There are developed campsites here.)

12.2 Cross SR 40 and then follow a boardwalk over marshland.

16.4 Cross FR 599.

20.2 Reach junction with the 0.1-mile blue-blazed trail to Farles Prairie Campground. (**FYI:** Water and latrines are available at the campground.)

20.8 Cross Forest Road 535.

22.3 Cross Forest Road 562.

22.6 Reach junction with the 0.5-mile blue-blazed trail to Buck Lake campsite.

23.9 Cross CR 9277.

24.8 Cross paved SR 19.

25.7 Cross FR 525.

27.4 Cross FR 445.

28.0 Cross FR 538.

28.2 Reach junction with the 0.5-mile blue blazed trail to Alexander Springs Campground.

30.0 Cross Forest Road 538A.

31.7 Traverse a long boardwalk before crossing FR 539. Then follow several short boardwalks through another swamp.

33.5 Cross power line right-of-way, and then cross a creek on a boardwalk.

36.5 Cross FR 538.

38.0 Reach junction with 0.3-mile blue-blazed trail to Clearwater Lake Campground.

38.4 Arrive at CR 42, the southern boundary of Ocala National Forest and the end of your hike.

28 Withlacoochee State Forest: Citrus Perimeter Loop

Meadows of saw palmetto stretch throughout much of the Central Florida terrain.

This forest takes its name from the Withlacoochee River, which meanders for 13 miles through the area. As Florida's third-largest state forest, it comprises 157,479 acres and spans four counties: Citrus, Pasco, Hernando, and Sumter. It's divided into eight tracts; this hike covers one of the most popular: the Citrus Tract, 42,531 acres. The World Wildlife Fund has called Withlacoochee "One of the 10 Coolest Places in North America You've Never Seen," but about 300,000 people do visit annually.

Start: Holder Mine Recreation Area parking area

Distance: 40.5-mile loop based on four stacked loops

Approximate hiking time: 3 to 4 days

Difficulty: Moderate due to length

Trail surface: Natural path

Seasons: Fall through spring but usually closed to hiking during hunting seasons—see "Special considerations" below

Other trail users: Hunters; no bikes or horses allowed

Canine compatibility: Leashed pets permitted

Land status: State forest

Nearest town: Inverness

Fees and permits: Daily user fee under $5; permit required for overnight camping, $7 for primitive camping sites

Schedule: Open dawn to dusk; closures occur during hunting season; details available from the visitor center. Visitor center (located on U.S. Highway 41 about 7 miles north of Brooksville) open 8:00 a.m. to 5:00 p.m. weekdays, 8:00 a.m. to noon and 12:30 to 4:30 p.m. on Saturday; closed Sunday

Maps: Available from the Forestry Visitor Center and the Florida Trail Association (FTA)

Trail contact: Withlacoochee State Forest, Recreation/Visitor Center, 15003 Broad Street, Brooksville, FL 34601; (352) 754-6896; www .fl-dof.com/state_forests/withlacoochee.html

Special considerations: The Citrus Tract is usually closed to hiking during the muzzle-loading season and part of the modern gun hunting season. During hunts, hikers should wear 500 square inches of blaze-orange clothing above the waist, and it must be visible in both front and back. Hunting schedule is available at www.myfwc.com/hunting.

Finding the trailhead: Holder Mine Recreation Area, near Inverness, is the usual starting point for hikes in the Citrus Tract. From State Road 44 in Inverness, go south on County Road 581 for 2 miles. The turnoff to the recreation area is on the right. Follow Forest Road 10 (also T10) for 2 miles to the parking area and trailhead kiosk.

The Hike

This hike is made up of four stacked loops, but we'll describe only the extended perimeter trail. As the map shows, there are several ways to shorten the multi-day hike into a day or single overnight walk, if you like.

Wildlife on this dry, all-weather trail includes deer, quail, foxes, and fox squirrels. The trail passes through areas of sandhill scrub, oak thickets, and stands of sand pine and longleaf pine. The eye-popping colors of wildflowers grace the landscape off and on from spring through fall. You'll also encounter a number of sinkholes on this alternately hilly and flat terrain.

▶ The state of Florida maintains a herd of longhorn cattle on the Richloam Tract. They are apparently descended from cattle introduced by early Spanish settlers.

The northernmost access to the 40-mile perimeter trail is the Holder Mine Recreation Area. The blue-blazed access trail goes past a sawdust pile and then intersects the A Loop trail at the end of the first mile. The junction with the blue-blazed A and B Loop cross trail is at Mile 5.2.

Continuing, you'll reach the junction with the blue-blazed cross trails for B and C Loops at Mile 14.7. Cross-trail junctions for C and D Loops come in at Mile 19.3 and again at Mile 31. You'll reach the access trail that comes in from the Mutual Mine Recreation Area at Mile 33. From that point, it's only another 7 miles back to your starting point at the Holder Mine Recreation Area.

Primitive camping is permitted within designated camping zones marked by white-banded trees. These are situated south of Mansfield Pond, west of Savage Pond, and between forest trails 8 and 10-A. Improved camping facilities are available at the Holder Mine and Mutual Mine trailheads and the Tillis Hill Recreation Area.

A trail for horses is marked with blue bands around the trees. Remain on the orange-blazed route, which also intersects the blue-blazed side trails.

Miles and Directions

0.0   Start at Holder Mine Recreation Area. Look for blue-blazed access trail on the western side of the parking area.

0.9   Reach junction with A Loop trail.

3.0   Cross T6, a paved road.

3.1   Pass Bull Sink.

5.2   Reach junction with the blue-blazed 1.6-mile cross trail for A and B Loops. Go right to join the B Loop.

7.0   Pass a cistern.

12.2   Pass junction with 0.2-mile side trail to a primitive camping area.

14.7   Reach junction of B and C Loops and the 1.6-mile cross trail coming from the left. Go straight to join C Loop.

16.6   Pass another primitive camping area.

16.8   Cross T15 Road.

19.3   Reach junction of C and D Loops and the 1.8-mile cross trail. Go right to join D Loop.

23.2   Pass Lizzie Hart Sink.

25.0   Cross County Road 480.

26.0   Cross T3 Road.

26.3   Pass a primitive camping area.

28.0   Cross CR 480.

31.5   Reach junction with C and D Loops. Go right to join C Loop.

32.2   Cross an old railroad grade.

32.8   Reach junction of C Loop and the 1.5-mile access trail to Mutual Mine Recreation Area, a developed camping area. Bear left to stay on C Loop.

33.4   Cross old railroad grade.

37.4   Reach junction of B and C Loop. Turn right onto B Loop.

38.9   At the junction of A and B Loops, turn right to rejoin A Loop.

39.7   Go right at junction with access trail to return to Holder Mine Recreation Area.

40.5   Arrive back at Holder Mine Recreation Area.

More Information

Local Information

Citrus County Chamber of Commerce: www.citruscountychamber.com/tourism.html.
Hernando County Chamber of Commerce: www.co.hernando.fl.us/visit.
Pasco County Tourism Development Council: http://visitpasco.net.

Local Events/Attractions

In addition to the described hikes, additional trails are available in the 2,500-acre Homosassa Tract and 2,896-acre Two Mile Prairie Tract. The visitor center has maps and directions.

Lodging

Lodging is available in Dade City, Zephyrhills, and Brooksville: http://visitpasco.net.

Camping

Camping is permitted in designated zones only. No open fires are permitted, only cook fires, and even these may be restricted during dry conditions.

Organizations

Florida Department of Agriculture and Consumer Services, Division of Forestry: www.fl-dof.com/state _forests.
West Pasco Audubon Society: www.westpascoaudubon.com.

FOX SQUIRRELS

The Sherman's fox squirrel is a large squirrel easily identified by its black head. Fox squirrels like forested areas that are fairly open so that when they're feeding on the ground they can spot predators at a distance and have plenty of time to escape up a tree. Fox squirrels are another declining species due to habitat loss. Fox squirrel nests, usually made in the crook of branches of turkey oaks and similar trees, are easiest to spot in winter when the forest canopy is less thick. The nests are made of sticks, pine needles, and tree leaves. Chewed pine cones at the base of a tree is evidence of their presence. Other hikes where you should look for fox squirrels include Wekiwa Springs State Park (Hike 22) and Tosohatchee Wildlife Management Area (Hike 23). In the Withlacoochee State Forest, fox squirrels can be best seen in the sandhills of the Citrus and Croom Tracts.

29 Three Lakes Wildlife Management Area/ Prairie Lakes Unit: Linear Florida Trail

The effects of controlled burns don't have to be unsightly, as this portrait of a young pine tree at Three Lakes WMA demonstrates.

The WMA's extended trail of 25.3 miles is one of the longest wooded hikes in the central Florida region. The path first penetrates the heart of Three Lakes WMA, where most of the walking is level, but you may have to wade after heavy rains. Good wildlife viewing opportunities abound, particularly for white-tailed deer and sandhill cranes. After the first 10 miles, the path enters the Prairie Lakes Unit of Three Lakes, which is the longer trail section and an area famous for its number of bald eagle nests.

In addition to the linear through-section of the Florida Trail, the Prairie Lakes Unit also contains two loop walks, each about 5.5 miles. They are well worth hiking separately and are described in the next entry.

Nearest town: Kenansville
Start: Marked trailhead at U.S. Highway 441
Distance: Three Lakes Trail (WMA trail plus Prairie Lakes Loops), 25.3 miles one-way
Approximate hiking time: Two to four days
Difficulty: Easy to moderate, depending on wetness
Trail surface: Natural pathways, jeep roads
Seasons: Fall to spring; public hunting area; hunting calendar is available at www.myfwc .com/hunting
Other trail users: Hunters in season
Canine compatibility: Pets prohibited
Land status: State wildlife management area
Fees and permits: No fees or permits required for through hikers; daily-use permit or Wildlife

Management Area permit required for other users
Schedule: Open dawn until sunset daily
Maps: Available online from the Florida Fish and Wildlife Conservation Commission and from the Florida Trail Association (FTA)
Trail contact: Florida Fish and Wildlife Conservation Commission, Central Region, 1239 Southwest Tenth Street, Ocala, FL 32674; (352) 732-1225; www.floridaconservation.org/ recreation/three_lakes/recreation.asp#Hiking
Special considerations: This is a public hunting area. During hunts, hikers should wear 500 square inches of blaze-orange clothing above the waist, and it must be visible in both front and back. Hunting schedule is available at www.myfwc.com/hunting.

Finding the trailhead: From Kenansville go north on US 441 for 8.3 miles to the official start of the hike. Look for the Florida Trail sign on the side of the road. (Overnight parking here is not recommended.) Enter the northern end of the WMA to park in the designated area. That not only cuts 2.5 miles from the hike, but your vehicle will be in a more secure place. **GPS:** N28 08.082' W081 04.350'

The Hike

This 25.3-mile linear hike passes through the length of the Three Lakes Wildlife Management Area and the Prairie Lakes Unit, part of the Kissimmee Prairie and one of the nation's largest remaining sections of dry prairie. Three Lakes is named for the three nearby bodies of water, Lakes Kissimmee, Jackson, and Marian.

If you start from US 441, you'll pass several sand forest roads, pass the Three Lakes Camp, and reach Williams Road. Williams Road will take you beneath the Florida Turnpike. You'll move on and off Williams Road via a jeep road. Williams Road eventually takes you to County Road 523, which leads to the Prairie Lakes Unit entrance (Mile 9.9).

From here, the Three Lakes Trail "borrows" about half of each of the two Prairie Lakes loop trails. If you like what you see here (pine forest, hammock, and marsh) it's possible to make a complete 11.1-mile circuit of the two loops. Or you can continue to the WMA's lower boundary, a total of 15.3 miles on the southern side of CR 523.

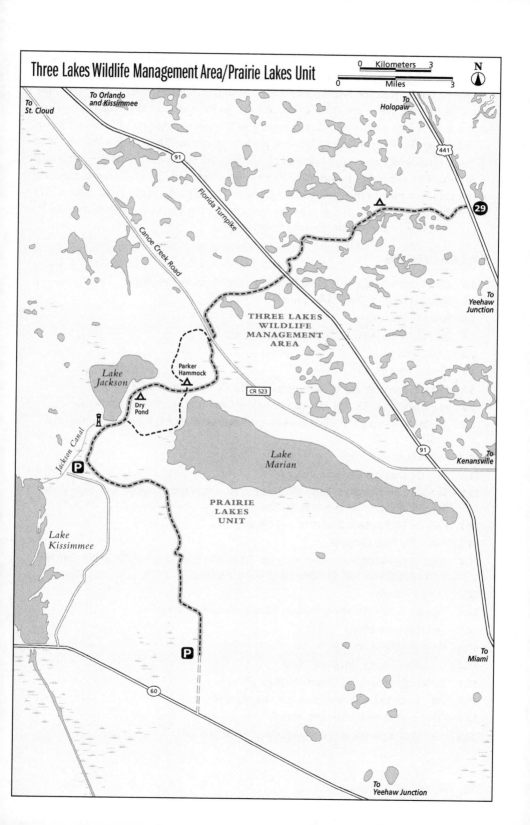

The walk includes hardwood and sabal palm hammocks, as well as some fairly open prairie. Spiked green palmetto palms are mixed in with the pines.

About a mile into the South Loop, you'll have the chance to take a short 0.6-mile side trail mile to the observation tower at Lake Jackson, one of the area's two prime scenic overlooks. Completing that detour, you'll continue right on the South Loop, soon exiting the Prairie Lakes Unit but remaining within Three Lakes WMA. After taking a road bridge to cross Fodderstock Slough, the trail passes both the north and south edges of Godwin Hammock. After a short jeep road, the trail crosses a prairie of nothing but spiked green palmettos. (*Caution:* This is prime rattlesnake habitat.) It's impossible to put blazes on this type of vegetation, so in places the trail is marked by a series of posts in this short-cropped green jungle.

Miles and Directions

0.0 Start by crossing the fence at the Three Lakes WMA boundary on US 441.

3.6 Pass a side trail to Three Lakes Camp.

4.6 Reach Williams Road.

6.4 Pass under the Florida Turnpike on Williams Road.

7.6 Cross Road 3.

8.1 Cross a stream.

9.2 Reach the junction with the WMA gate and CR 523. Go left on CR 523.

9.7 At the junction of CR 523 and Prairie Lake Road, turn right onto Prairie Lake Road.

9.9 Join the North Loop of the Florida Trail in the Prairie Lakes Unit. Turn left to follow the main FNST.

10.3 Pass a high-water route.

11.4 Pass the road to a fire tower.

12.2 Reach the junction of the North and South Loops at the Road 16 bridge. Turn left to follow the FNST and the west side of South Loop.

13.5 Pass the Lake Jackson boat ramp and camping area.

13.7 Reach Dry Pond campsite.

15.4 South Loop intersects the linear main trail. Go straight to follow the FNST. (**Option:** Turn left to make loop walk back to Prairie Lakes Unit entrance.)

16.3 Cross a fenceline.

16.4 Pass a 0.6-mile side trail to the Lake Jackson observation tower.

16.9 Go left at a fenceline.

17.0 Cross a stile and Road 16.

18.3 Cross Fodderstack Slough via bridge.

18.6 Go straight at the trail junction with Road 10.

21.1 Pass a side trail to Godwin Hammock camping area.

22.7 Go straight at the junction with Road 9.

25.3 Hike ends at parking area on Three Lakes WMA access road.

Note: The entry Prairie Lakes Unit: North and South Loop Trails describes the Prairie Lakes segment of the Three Lakes Wildlife Management Area.

More Information

Local Information

Kissimmee/Osceola County Chamber of Commerce: www.kissimmeechamber.com.
Kissimmee Convention & Visitors Bureau: www.floridakiss.com.

Local Events/Attractions

Lakes Jackson, Marian, and Kissimmee offer canoeing and kayaking opportunities.

Prairie Lakes Unit contains a 7-mile interpretive drive. A printed guide is available at the entrance kiosk.

Lodging

Lodging is available in Holopaw and St. Cloud.

Camping

Primitive campsites are available in both the Wildlife Management Area and Prairie Lakes. You must obtain a camping permit in advance for Prairie Lakes: (352) 732-1225. Camping is restricted in both areas during hunting season; check the schedule before you go.

Organizations

Florida Fish and Wildlife Conservation Commission: http://myfwc.com.

30 Prairie Lakes Unit: North and South Loop Trails

Bald eagles frequently nest near the Prairie Lakes Unit trailhead.

The two loop trails of the Prairie Lakes unit are part of the Florida Trail system and join the through trail at the end of the South Loop. Hike them separately or hike both of them, or make them a part of a very long haul by hiking them in addition to the Linear Florida Trail.

Nearest town: Kenansville
Start: Shared trailhead of North and South Loops
Distance: North Loop, 5.5-mile loop; South Loop, 5.6-mile loop

Approximate hiking time: North Loop, 3 hours; South Loop, 4 hours
Difficulty: Easy to moderate, depending on wetness
Trail surface: Primarily natural surface

Seasons: Fall to spring

Other trail users: Hunters in season

Canine compatibility: Pets prohibited

Land status: State land

Fees and permits: No fees or permits required for through hikers; daily-use permit or Wildlife Management Area permit required for other users

Schedule: Open dawn until sunset daily

Maps: Available online from the Florida Fish and Wildlife Conservation Commission and from the Florida Trail Association (FTA)

Trail contact: Florida Fish and Wildlife Conservation Commission, Central Region, 1239 Southwest Tenth Street, Ocala, FL 32674; (352) 732-1225

Finding the trailhead: Take SR 523 (Canoe Creek Road) to the Prairie Lakes Unit. Turn south onto Prairie Lakes Road and park at the designated area, the common trailhead for the North and South Loops. If you hiked the first part of Three Lakes, you'll be entering the Prairie Lakes Unit on Prairie Lakes Road after crossing CR 523/Canoe Creek Road. **GPS:** Lake Marian, N27 55.650' W081 07.494'

The Hikes

North Loop

Going left on the 5.5-mile North Loop, the trail skirts cypress ponds where bald eagles frequently nest. Outside of Alaska, Florida has more nesting bald eagles than any other state in the nation. Florida's bald eagles nest at a time contrary to that in other parts of the country. Elsewhere, bald eagles nest in the spring and summer because food is at its most abundant. Florida eagles, on the other hand, nest in winter when prey here is most plentiful, in the dry winter season. When ponds shrink or dry up, fish are more concentrated and easier to locate.

In wet conditions, you may also need to take the high water route to pass through the area.

These loops, or even just sections of them, can also be part of a longer, multiday hike, Three Lakes Wildlife Management Area/Prairie Lakes Unit: Linear Florida Trail, also described in this book.

Miles and Directions

0.0 From parking area on Prairie Lakes Road, bear left to join the North Loop. This section is also part of the Florida Trail through segment.

0.4 Pass a high-water route.

1.5 Pass the road to a fire tower.

3.1 North Loop junctions with South Loop. Day parking and camping available. To continue on the North Loop, bear to extreme right.

5.6 Arrive back at North Loop trailhead parking lot.

South Loop

Bear right on the 5.6-mile South Loop, which will take you near Lake Jackson, a

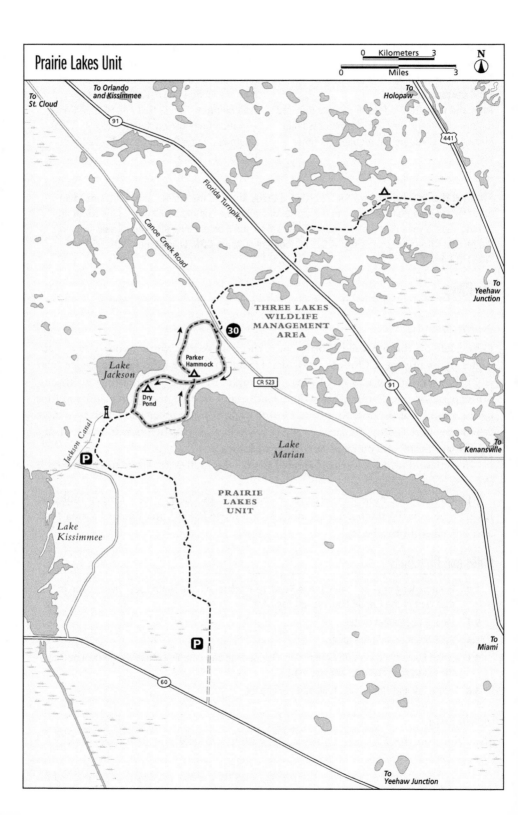

Prairie Lakes Unit

To
St. Cloud

To Orlando
and Kissimmee

To
Holopaw

91

441

Florida Turnpike

Canoe Creek Road

To
Yeehaw
Junction

THREE LAKES
WILDLIFE
MANAGEMENT
AREA

30

Parker
Hammock

Lake
Jackson

Dry
Pond

CR 523

91

Jackson Canal

Lake
Marian

To
Kenansville

P

Lake
Kissimmee

PRAIRIE
LAKES
UNIT

P

To
Miami

60

To
Yeehaw Junction

popular fishing area. As you walk south, your path will encounter boat ramps and use more bridges. In about a mile you'll reach the short 0.6-mile side trail to the observation tower at Lake Jackson, one of the area's two prime scenic overlooks. Next, you'll pass the Lake Jackson boat ramp and then the Dry Pond campsite, 1.5 miles from where the North/South loops junction. In just 2 more miles the South Loop joins the main FNST. Bear to the extreme left to return to the North/South loop junction.

Miles and Directions

0.0 From parking area at North/South loop trail junction, begin South Loop, bearing left toward Lake Jackson.

0.9 Cross a fenceline.

1.0 Pass a 0.6-mile side trail to the Lake Jackson observation tower.

1.2 Pass the Lake Jackson boat ramp and camping area.

1.5 Reach Dry Pond campsite.

3.2 South Loop crosses Florida Trail. Bear extreme left and go northeast to continue on South Loop.

5.6 Arrive back at South/North Loop trail junction and parking lot.

More Information

Local Information

Kissimmee/Osceola County Chamber of Commerce: www.kissimmeechamber.com.
Kissimmee Convention & Visitors Bureau: www.floridakiss.com.

Local Events/Attractions

Lakes Jackson, Marian, and Kissimmee offer canoeing and kayaking opportunities.
Prairie Lakes Unit contains a 7-mile interpretive drive. A printed guide is available at the entrance kiosk.

Lodging

Lodging is available in Holopaw and St. Cloud.

Camping

Primitive campsites are available in both the Wildlife Management Area and Prairie Lakes. You must obtain a camping permit in advance for Prairie Lakes: (352) 732-1225. Camping is restricted in both areas during hunting season; check the schedule before you go.

Organizations

Florida Fish and Wildlife Conservation Commission: http://myfwc.com.

Hiker's Checklist

The "best" way to realize the importance of a good checklist is being on a wilderness trail about 15 miles from the trailhead and discover that you have forgotten an important item. The thing you forgot may be only an inconvenience, or it may be seriously important. A good checklist will help prevent your forgetting the things you need to make your hike safe and enjoyable.

This is only a suggested list. Base your list on the nature of the hike and your own personal needs. Items will vary depending on whether you are camping near your vehicle or backpacking to more remote campsites and staying out one or more nights. Remember, if you are carrying it on your back, select items judiciously. Weight is an important factor.

Check each item as you pack.

Day Hike Checklist

- ❏ Polarized sunglasses
- ❏ Waterproof sunblock
- ❏ Insect repellent
- ❏ Hat with full brim
- ❏ Compass and map of hiking area
- ❏ Fanny pack with snacks and two water bottles
- ❏ Cell phone in case of emergency
- ❏ Bandages for blisters
- ❏ Ankle support device in case of sprain
- ❏ First-aid kit with tweezers
- ❏ For thick mosquito country or prolonged sun exposure, lightweight long-sleeved shirt and long pants
- ❏ Dry clothes back at your vehicle in case of rain
- ❏ Ice chest with cold drinks in vehicle for your return

For Extended Hikes

All of the above plus the following items:

- ❏ GPS
- ❏ Flashlight with spare batteries
- ❏ Water-sterilizing tablets or portable water purifier
- ❏ Dusting powder for groin and feet
- ❏ Commercial rehydrating salts
- ❏ Antidiarrhetic
- ❏ Laxative (we all react differently)
- ❏ Aspirin

Index

About the Author

Tim O'Keefe, a past president of the Florida Outdoor Writers Association and a member of the Florida Trail Association, has lived in the Orlando area since 1968. For almost three decades, his articles and photographs have appeared in numerous publications, including eight National Geographic Society books, *Men's Journal, National Geographic Traveler, Discovery Channel Online, Outside, Caribbean Travel & Life, Newsweek, Sport Diver,* the *New York Times,* and the *Chicago Tribune.*

His new Web site, www.FloridaWild lifeViewing.com, brings together all of his Florida outdoor experiences. His other love and expertise is the Caribbean, with his insights available at www .GuideToCaribbeanVacations.com (GTCV.com) and www.caribbeanhik ing.com.

Tim was a major contributor to the *National Geographic Guide to Caribbean Family Vacations.* He also authored *Caribbean Hiking; The Spicy Camp Cook Book; Seasonal Guide to the Natural Year: Florida with Georgia and Alabama Coasts; Great Adventures in Florida; Manatees, Our Vanishing Mermaids; Sea Turtles: The Watcher's Guide; Fish and Dive the Caribbean* and *Fish and Dive Florida & The Keys* (both with Larry Larsen); *Diving to Adventure;* and AAA's *A Photo Journey to Central Florida.*

Tim's work has won more than fifty regional and national awards. *The Spicy Camp Cook Book* and *Seasonal Guide to the Natural Year: Florida with Georgia and Alabama Coasts* were named Best Book by the Florida Outdoor Writers Association. Tim has published more than 15,000 photographs worldwide.

He received a Ph.D. from the University of North Carolina at Chapel Hill. Before retiring to freelance full time, he was a professor and head of the journalism division in the Nicholson School of Communication at the University of Central Florida, where he established the journalism program.

Lightning Source UK Ltd.
Milton Keynes UK
UKHW021304090223
416759UK00038B/668

9 780762 743544